5th Celtic Language Technology Workshop (CLTW 5)

Held online

Abu Dhabi, United Arab Emirates
20 January 2025

ISBN: 979-8-3313-1362-3

Printed from e-media with permission by:

Curran Associates, Inc.
57 Morehouse Lane
Red Hook, NY 12571

Some format issues inherent in the e-media version may also appear in this print version.

Printed with permission by Curran Associates, Inc. (2026)

Association for Computational Linguistics
209 N. Eighth Street
Stroudsburg, Pennsylvania 18360

Phone: 1-570-476-8006
Fax: 1-570-476-0860

acl@aclweb.org

Additional copies of this publication are available from:

Curran Associates, Inc.
57 Morehouse Lane
Red Hook, NY 12571 USA
Phone: 845-758-0400
Fax: 845-758-2633
Email: curran@proceedings.com
Web: www.proceedings.com

COLING

Celtic Language Technology Workshop

Proceedings of the 5th Workshop (CLTW 5)

January 20, 2025
Abu Dhabi, UAE (Online)

Preface

These proceedings include the programme and papers presented at the 5th Celtic Language Technology Workshop (CLTW 5), co-located with COLING, Abu Dhabi, January 19–24, 2025. The fifth edition has been organised as a virtual event to allow for higher attendance to the workshop.

In classical antiquity, Celtic languages were spoken across much of present-day Eurasia. In modern times, Celtic languages survive primarily in select regions of the United Kingdom, France, and Ireland, while also finding homes in diaspora communities in Argentina and Canada. The surviving Celtic languages comprise Welsh, Irish, Scottish Gaelic, Manx, Breton, and Cornish.

While these languages have relatively small speaker populations compared to major European languages, they maintain strong cultural and social significance in their traditional territories and urban areas. Among them, Irish holds a distinctive position as the only Celtic language with full European Union official status, achieved in 2007. Welsh, Gaelic, and Manx enjoy co-official recognition in their respective regions, while Breton and Cornish receive limited official acknowledgment in their historical territories.

A significant challenge facing all Celtic languages is their historical lack of resources and natural language processing (NLP) applications, which are crucial for maintaining relevance in our digital age. However, the landscape has begun to shift positively in recent years. These languages are increasingly benefiting from new academic and technological initiatives designed to support under-resourced languages. Dedicated research teams now focus on developing language and speech processing technologies for Celtic languages.

A significant milestone in this development was the establishment of CLTW. With the fifth edition, CLTW celebrates its tenth anniversary—the first workshop was held exactly ten years ago, also at COLING (Dublin 2014). Over the last ten years, this forum has served as a vital platform for researchers to collaborate, share innovative work, and elevate the profile of Celtic language technology in the global linguistic community.

Despite a lower submission rate than previous years and an exclusive focus on Scottish Gaelic and Irish this time, the accepted papers in this edition represent an interesting mix of work; they cover automatic speech recognition (ASR), game-based learning, the use of LLMs for text expansion and translation, and tokenisation for Old Irish.

We thank our invited speakers for their valuable contributions: Linda Heimisdóttir (Miðeind, Reykjavík, Iceland) and Dr. Alham Fikri Aji (Mohamed bin Zayed University of Artificial Intelligence, Abu Dhabi, UAE). We also extend our gratitude to all presenters for their hard work and to the workshop attendees for their active participation. Finally, we are deeply grateful to our program committee members for their thorough reviews and invaluable feedback on the published work.

The CLTW 5 Organisers,
Brian Davis, Theodorus Fransen, Elaine Uí Dhonnchadha, and Abigail Walsh

Program Committee

Colin Batchelor, Royal Society of Chemistry, UK

Inge Birnie, University of Strathclyde, UK

Alan Cowap, Dublin City University, Ireland

Adrian Doyle, Insight SFI Centre for Data Analytics, Data Science Institute, University of Galway, Ireland

Johannes Heinecke, Orange Innovation, France

Mélanie Jouitteau, CNRS, France

John Judge, ADAPT Centre, Dublin City University, Ireland

Dawn Knight, Cardiff University, UK

William Lamb, The University of Edinburgh, UK

John P. McCrae, Insight SFI Centre for Data Analytics, Data Science Institute, University of Galway, Ireland

Simon Mille, ADAPT Centre, Dublin City University, Ireland

Caoimhín Ó Donnaíle, Sabhal Mòr Ostaig UHI, UK

Paul Rayson, Lancaster University, UK

Kevin Scannell, Cadhan Aonair, LLC, St. Louis, Missouri, USA

Monica Ward, Dublin City University, Ireland

David Willis, University of Oxford, UK

Organising Committee

Brian Davis, ADAPT Centre, Dublin City University, Ireland

Theodorus Fransen, Università Cattolica del Sacro Cuore, Milan, Italy

Elaine Uí Dhonnchadha, Trinity College Dublin, Ireland

Abigail Walsh, ADAPT Centre, Dublin City University, Ireland

Invited Speakers

Linda Heimisdóttir, Miðeind, Reykjavík, Iceland

Alham Fikri Aji, Mohamed bin Zayed University of Artificial Intelligence, Abu Dhabi, UAE

Table of Contents

Conference Program

09:00 ***UTC+0–09:10 Welcome***

09:10–09:50 *Keynote Speech*
Linda Heimisdóttir, CEO of Miðeind, a leader in language technology and artificial intelligence for Icelandic

09:50–10:15 *An Assessment of Word Separation Practices in Old Irish Text Resources and a Universal Method for Tokenising Old Irish Text*
Adrian Doyle and John P. McCrae

10:15–10:35 ***Break***

10:35–11:00 *Synthesising a Corpus of Gaelic Traditional Narrative with Cross-Lingual Text Expansion*
William Lamb, Dongge Han, Ondrej Klejch, Beatrice Alex and Peter Bell

11:00–11:25 *A Pragmatic Approach to Using Artificial Intelligence and Virtual Reality in Digital Game-Based Language Learning*
Monica Ward, Liang Xu and Elaine Uí Dhonnchadha

11:25–11:45 ***Break***

11:45–12:25 *Keynote Speech*
Dr. Alham Fikri Aji, Mohamed bin Zayed University of Artificial Intelligence, Abu Dhabi, UAE

12:25–12:50 *Fotheidil: an Automatic Transcription System for the Irish Language*
Liam Lonergan, Ibon Saratxaga, John Sloan, Oscar Maharg Bravo, Mengjie Qian, Neasa Ní Chiaráin, Christer Gobl and Ailbhe Ní Chasaide

12:50–13:15 *Gaeilge Bhriste ó Shamhlacha Cliste: How Clever Are LLMs When Translating Irish Text?*
Teresa Clifford, Abigail Walsh, Brian Davis and Mícheál J. Ó Meachair

13:15–13:25 *Concluding Remarks*
CLTW Committee

An Assessment of Word Separation Practices in Old Irish Text Resources and a Universal Method for Tokenising Old Irish Text

Adrian Doyle and **John P. McCrae**
Insight SFI Centre for Data Analytics
Data Science Institute
University of Galway
adrian.odubhghaill@universityofgalway.ie and john@mccr.ae

Abstract

The quantity of Old Irish text which survives in contemporary manuscripts is relatively small by comparison to what is available for well-resourced modern languages. Moreover, as it is a historical language, no more text will ever be generated by native speakers of Old Irish. This makes the text which has survived particularly valuable, and ideally, all of it would be annotated using a single, common annotation standard, thereby ensuring compatibility between text resources. At present, Old Irish text repositories separate words or sub-word morphemes in accordance with different methodologies, and each uses a different style of lexical annotation. This makes it difficult to utilise content from more than any one repository in NLP applications. This paper provides an assessment of distinctions between existing annotated corpora, showing that the primary point of divergence is at the token level. For this reason, this paper also describes a new method for tokenising Old Irish text. This method can be applied even to diplomatic editions, and has already been utilised in various text resources.

1 Introduction

The majority of text which survives in contemporary Old Irish manuscripts has already been digitised and lexically annotated. This content is available online from various text repositories. Methods used for separating and annotating words and morphemes differ between repositories, however, with the result that data is incompatible between existing repositories. As interest in the application of various NLP techniques to historical Irish texts increases, several sources have reported that experiments were impacted by the lack of standardisation between text resources such as these (Doyle et al., 2019; Doyle and McCrae, 2024; Dereza et al., 2023a,b). Regarding digital resources for Gaelic languages, Stifter et al. found that "The most pressing issues include lack of standardisation and agreement of norms ... and inconsistency as far as tokenisation and use of unique identifiers across various Gaelic resources" (2021b, 8), which they suggest "can cause confusion and hinders linkage and interoperability." Moreover, Dereza et al. concluded that "the necessity of a text editing standard, especially for NLP applications, has not been properly debated and investigated by the historical Irish academic community" (2023a, 86).

This paper addresses the lack of standardisation among Old Irish text resources. It will demonstrate some of the main ways that text data and lexical annotations differ between existing resources in section 2, and will discuss some of the grammatical and orthographic reasons such distinctions exist. It will be shown that diplomatic editions, those in which editors attempt to faithfully reproduce text as it appeared in an original manuscript, can cause particular difficulty for Old Irish word separation. A novel method for tokenising diplomatically edited Old Irish text, which can prevent lexical variation between tokenised corpora, will be presented in section 3. It will be demonstrated that this method can also be applied to normalised, or otherwise altered text. Finally, section 4 will discuss how this tokenisation method has allowed for the consistent annotation of distinct Old Irish text resources, ensuring compatibility between them.

2 Currently Available Corpora

The historical stage of the Irish language as it was written between roughly the 7th and 9th centuries is termed Old Irish. Many texts which may be described linguistically as Old Irish can be found in manuscripts which date from later than the 9th century, having been copied from earlier sources. As Stokes and Strachan note, however, "Middle-Irish transcribers have often modernised or corrupted these ancient documents" (1901, xi). For this reason, the corpus of Old Irish text which survives in

Proceedings of the 5th Celtic Language Technology Workshop (CLTW 5), pages 1–11
Abu Dhabi, UAE (Online), January 20, 2025

Examples	Source	Text Ref.	Raw Text	Words
1a	**SGP**	Sg. 1b1	".i. ci insamlar"	"ci", "in", "in·samlar"
1b	**CorPH**	Sg. 1b1	".i. ci in·samlar"	".i.", "ci'", "in·", "in·samlar"
2a	**SGP**	Sg. 7b8	"do·furgabtais"	"do", "fur", "-", "do·furgabtais"
2b	**CorPH**	Sg. 7b8	"do·furgabtais"	"do·", "·fur", "∅", "do·furgabtais"
3a	**MIDB**	Ml. 2b3	".i. dintsruth"	"di", "int", "sruth"
3b	**CorPH**	Ml. 2b3	".i. dintsruth"	"di", "int", "sruth"
4	**POMIC**	Arm. 64	–	"d-a-beir", "side", "0"

Table 1: Comparison of Old Irish raw text and word separation between various text repositories: **CorPH** (Stifter et al., 2021a), **MIDB** (Griffith, 2013), **POMIC** (Lash, 2014b), **SGP** (Bauer et al., 2023)

manuscripts dated to the Old Irish period itself is of particular value.

Compared to the total quantity of existing text which may be described as Old Irish, the contemporary Old Irish corpus is relatively small, and the types of texts which comprise it are more limited. A small amount of Old Irish prose and poetry survives in contemporary manuscripts, though the majority of the contemporary Old Irish corpus is comprised of glosses. These glosses can vary in length from a single word to several sentences, though the majority are quite short. Three large collections exist, the Würzburg (Wb.) glosses, the Milan (Ml.) glosses, and the St. Gall (Sg.) glosses. A significant amount of code-switching occurs between Old Irish and Latin in each of these collections, however, Ml. contains the largest quantity of Old Irish text with 8,443 glosses being collected for that corpus by Stifter et al. (2021a). Sg. has the least Irish content with 3,478 glosses according to e-codices (2005), meanwhile there are 3,501 Irish glosses in Wb. (Doyle, 2018).

Separate projects have been undertaken to digitise and annotate the three corpora of glosses (Griffith, 2013; Bauer, 2015; Bauer et al., 2023; Doyle, 2018). Two Universal Dependencies (UD) treebanks have since been created (Doyle, 2023a,b), each containing a small selection of these glosses. Otherwise, the *Parsed Old and Middle Irish Corpus* (POMIC; Lash, 2014b) contains some Old Irish prose text, and a variety of content has been collected and annotated in *Corpus PalaeoHibernicum* (CorPH; Stifter et al., 2021a). The resources discussed in section 4, which make use of the tokenisation method described here in section 3, use UD style part-of-speech (POS) tags (Zeman, 2016). Aside from these, though each of the remaining resources provide lexical annotation, only POMIC makes use of an established POS tag-set. According to Lash (2014a), POMIC uses a variety of Penn-style POS-tags (Santorini, 1990) which were originally adapted for use with Old English (Santorini, 2016). Each of the other resources utilise discrete lexical annotations.

The more noteworthy distinction between resources than lexical annotation, however, is that each separates words in accordance with different methods. Separating words is a deceptively difficult task for Old Irish (Doyle et al., 2019). While the orthographies of many modern European languages require spacing to occur between most words, for Old Irish "... words which are grouped round a single chief stress and have a close syntactic connexion with each other are written as one in the manuscripts" (Thurneysen, 1946, 24). Often this can result in word clusters which are difficult to separate. For example, where the words "*is*" and "*samlid*" come together, sometimes a letter is elided, forming a compound which is difficult to separate, "*isamlid*", 'it is thus', (as in Wb. 4a4 and 5b36). Occurrences of such clusters can result in different words being separated and annotated in different ways by different resources, even where they represent the same manuscript text.

A handful of examples of Old Irish text from various repositories can be found in Table 1. While an exhaustive list of distinctions between existing text repositories is not possible, these examples are sufficient to demonstrate some of the major differences between editorial standards and word separation methods used by each repository. The "Raw Text" column displays how each repository represents the text of the manuscript before applying word separation. POMIC (Lash, 2014b) is an exception as it does not contain pre-separation text data. The "Words" column displays the words iden-

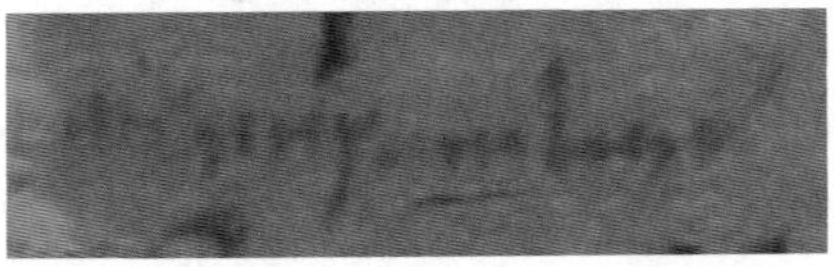

Figure 1: *.i.ciinsamlar* (1b1) from St. Gallen, Stiftsbibliothek, Cod. Sang. 904 (`www.e-codices.ch`).

Figure 2: *dofurgabtais* (7b8) from St. Gallen, Stiftsbibliothek, Cod. Sang. 904 (`www.e-codices.ch`).

tified by each repository after separation.

Examples 1a and 1b demonstrate that the raw text can differ between repositories based on editorial decisions. In the case of 1b the editors have supplied punctuation in "*ci in·samlar*" ('if I should imitate') which was not supplied by the editors of the exact same text, "*ci insamlar*", in example 1a. Though faded, it can just about be seen in Figure 1 that no punctuation occurs in the original manuscript either. Similarly, while the editors of both 2a and 2b supply punctuation in the raw text, "*do·furgabtais*" ('they should enunciate'), it can be seen in Figure 2 that no such punctuation appears in the manuscript. Because of editorial distinctions such as this, a tokenisation method for Old Irish will need to be capable of handling text both with and without this manner of punctuation. For this same reason it is currently a requirement that Old and Middle Irish treebanks added to UD must be identified as either "diplomatic" or "critical", where "diplomatic" treebanks cannot include punctuation, capitalisation or other text characters inserted by editors (with the exception of expanded abbreviations), unless they appear in the manuscript[1].

Further distinctions between resources become apparent when examining how words are separated. Even where text has been drawn from a single source, and the raw text is identical, different repositories will often separate different words. For example, 2a has "*do*", "*fur*" and "-" equating to "*do·*", "*·fur*" and "∅" in 2b. There is also a tendency among resources for separated words not to reflect the raw text character-for-character, making it impossible to reproduce the raw text by simply concatenating the separated words. In 3a and 3b, for example, only a single *i* occurs in the raw text, "*di̱ntsruth*" ('from the torrent'), however, concatenating the words identified by each resource, "*di*" ('from') and "*int*" ('the'), would result in "*di̱i̱ntsruth*" with two *i*s. More egregiously, in 2b where the raw text reads "*do·furgabtais*", concatenating the words identified by the resource would result in the gibberish string "*do··fur∅do·furgabtais*". In three examples, 2a, 2b, and 4, an "empty" word is supplied to represent a semantic element which is understood to occur in that position, but not represented in the raw text. This duplication and addition of characters is not typical of word-level tokenisation but is common in Old Irish resources, particularly where an attempt is made separate the verbal complex into its various components, while also portraying it as a single word. In stark contrast, example 4 presents the entire verbal complex, "*d-a-beir*" ('he gives it'), as a single word only. While this is more representative of typical tokenisation practice, hyphenation which would not have occurred in the manuscript was introduced to identify the infixed pronoun, "*-a-*" ('it') from the rest of the verb. As such, this word separation method necessitates altering the original text for clarity.

As a comparison is being drawn here between the separation of words in various Old Irish text repositories and what might be typically expected of tokenisation, it must be noted that only Lash (2014a) actually uses the term "tokens" in the annotation manual for *POMIC*, and only once. Otherwise, he generally refers to "words" and "word-division", while other resources use the terms "phonolog[ical] word" (Griffith, 2013), "word form" (Bauer et al., 2023), and "morph" (Stifter et al., 2021a). This reflects the fact that these resources were not necessarily developed to be used in NLP applications, but as aides to linguistic research. Griffith (2013), for example, describes the Ml. database as a "dictionary" and a "lexicon" rather than as an annotated digital text. It would therefore be unreasonable to expect word division in these repositories to reflect tokenisation in a traditional sense. Indeed, the methods used by each

[1]Conversely, any treebank containing editorial alterations to the text such as these must be identified as "critical", though this definition does not align perfectly with the common use of the term "critical edition". For more information see discussion of Treebank Classification at `https://universaldependencies.org/sga/index.html`.

resource for separating words, and sometimes also smaller morphemes, are perfectly valid from a linguistic perspective, even though resources may differ from one another. If facilitating downstream NLP applications is to be treated as a realistic objective in the future development of Old Irish text resources, however, compatibility between these resources at the word level must be afforded more consideration than it has been to date. Identifying a single, universally applicable method for tokenising Old Irish text is clearly the first step which must be taken in this direction, as tokenisation necessarily impacts following steps like POS-tagging and dependency parsing. Such a tokenisation method will need to satisfy the requirements of both diplomatically edited manuscript text, and text which has been normalised or otherwise altered.

3 Tokenisation Method

The purpose of this section is to present a new tokenisation method which can be universally applied to all Old Irish text, be it diplomatically edited or altered by modern editors in any of a variety of ways (including silent word separation, expanding manuscript contractions and abbreviations, supplying capitalisation or punctuation, etc.). The main principles of this tokenisation method are as follows:

1. The character content of the raw text should not be altered by the tokenisation process, other than by the removal of whitespace characters between words.
2. Tokens (other than punctuation and symbols) resulting from the process should represent lexical words, not orthographic combinations made up of multiple parts-of-speech.
3. Tokens should represent synchronically Old Irish words, regardless of how such words may have developed diachronically.
4. No "empty/zero" characters should be introduced to represent lexemes which are not already represented in the raw text.
5. Resulting tokens should conform to the expectations of widely used text-data frameworks and POS-tagging schemes, such as UD.

For reasons of space, it would be impossible to provide a comprehensive discussion of every type of word here, however, detailed examples of the suggested tokenisation of various parts-of-speech can be found in Tables 2, 3, 4 and 5[2]. These can be found in Appendices A, B, C and D respectively.

3.1 Unproblematic Parts-of-speech

Many parts-of-speech are relatively unproblematic insofar as tokenisation is concerned, and can be separated relatively intuitively. Nouns like "*fer*" ('man'), "*ben*" ('woman') or "*guide*" ('prayer'), adjectives like "*becc*" ('small'), "*már*" ('large') or "*maith*" ('good'), and numerals like "*óen*" ('one'), "*cethir*" ('four') or "*secht*" ('seven'), are generally separated from surrounding words in modern editions and learning material using spacing, and this can be applied consistently with no further alteration typically occurring in the text as a result. Such parts-of-speech will always form discrete tokens of their own. A more complete list of parts-of-speech which can be separated into discrete tokens with relative ease can be found in Table 2.

While the parts-of-speech represented in Table 2 can be tokenised in a manner similar to most other languages, without any substantial linguistic disagreement, a few points should be noted about particular examples. Firstly, *olchena*, though it has a discrete entry in the *Electronic Dictionary of the Irish Language* (eDIL; Toner et al., 2019), is not considered an adverb in its own right, but a combination of *ol* and *cene*. This is necessary as the form occasionally occurs with spacing between these components in manuscript sources. In all other cases, adverbs form discrete tokens. Secondly, conjugating prepositions are treated as individual tokens in Old Irish treebanks. This is in line with Stifter's claims that these constitute "a single entity" (2006, 87) and that "It is not possible to separate one element from the other". It is also in line with the example of UD treebanks for Modern Irish, however, it should be noted that Scottish Gaelic and Manx Gaelic treebanks currently treat these as compounds of prepositions with pronouns.

3.2 Problematic Parts-of-speech

Consistent separation of words other than those in Table 2 can pose more difficulty, particularly where phenomena like syncope and apocope affect

[2]Discrete examples are separated by commas in these tables. Where a single example includes more than one token, the relevant token appears in bold and underlined. For example, where "***a*** *sind*" and "***do*** *nd*" appear as examples in Table 3 in the "Prepositions" row, the prepositions in these examples are "***a***" and "***do***" respectively. In such examples, spacing is used to separate all tokens, even where spacing may not have occurred in the raw text.

compounds of multiple words, but also in many other cases where shifting stress patterns affect the orthographic representation of clitics. Thurneysen claims "The absence of stress is most complete in (1) the article or a possessive pronoun standing between a preposition and the word it governs, (2) infixed pronouns and (sometimes) **ro** between preverbs and verbs, and (3) the copula between conjunctions and the predicate" (1946, 31). Indeed, the verbal complex, the article, the copula, and other words with which they can combine, are responsible for most of the difficulty in tokenising Old Irish. Table 3 demonstrates the suggested tokenisation for some of the more problematic parts-of-speech in Old Irish, other than those directly related to the verbal complex. Copula and Verb tokens, being some of the most problematic, are presented in Table 4, while other parts-of-speech which make up the verbal complex can be found in Table 5. Each of these tables demonstrate how tokens should be separated when they occur in compounds.

For many word-types represented in Table 3, separation is only problematic where they combine with other words. Independent personal pronouns like "*mé*" ('me'), and possessive pronouns like "*mo*" ('my'), for example, are not problematic to tokenise. Where they are compounded, however, producing forms like the "*mei-*" of "*meisse*" ('me!'), or the "*m-*" of "*móinur*" ('I alone'), knowing whether these should be separated can be less intuitive. Nevertheless, to enable the production of text resources in widely adopted formats, such as UD treebanks, a single, consistent tokenisation method must be applied in cases like these. It is the suggestion of this paper that all of the word types identified in Table 3 should be separated such that they form discrete tokens.

Certain conjunctions can be particularly problematic, especially in cases where what might be considered individual conjunctions can be found with spacing between their component morphemes in both manuscripts and learning material. Stifter, for example, lists "*in tain*" ('when'), "*íarsindí*" ('after'), "*fo bíth*" ('because'), "*in chruth*" ('so/as') and "*is cumme*" ('it is the same as if') as conjunctions (2006, 248–249), though it is suggested here that they be interpreted instead as multi-word expressions, and tokenised accordingly. To these, Stifter adds discrete negative forms of conjunctions like "*an(n)a*" ('while not'), "*arná*" ('so that not'), and the space-separated "*ol ní*" ('because not'). In accordance with this tokenisation method, these too should be separated to form discrete tokens. Conversely, certain items which should probably be considered discrete lexical conjunctions by the Old Irish period, like "*cenmitha*" ('aside from/in addition to'), can nevertheless be found written graphically as two words in manuscripts, "*cen mitha*" (see Sg. 150b3). Such cases present some difficulty for tokenisation as they require either that a lexical word be separated into sub-word morphemes, or that a space character can occur within a token, which is exceptional in UD treebanks. Nevertheless, the suggestion here is that conjunctions like "*cen mitha*" should be represented by a single token, even if that token contains a space character.

3.3 The Copula

The Copula deserves particular attention. The basic, non-combining forms (*"am", "at", "is"*, etc.) can be tokenised relatively easily. It becomes difficult, however, to systematically separate copula forms from certain other morphs which may be considered parts-of-speech in their own right. It is tempting, for example, to separate negative particles from what may be seen as copula endings ("*níta*" = "*ní*" + "*ta*"). As the third singular negative form "*ní*" contains no such ending in the orthography, however, no distinct copula token could result. For this reason, discrete negative copula forms should be retained as tokens for all persons and numbers (see Table 4).

3.4 The Verbal Complex

As the size of Table 5 might indicate, the verbal complex is the single feature in Old Irish orthography which creates the most difficulty for tokenisation. This can be ascribed to the sheer number of distinct types of words which can be compounded within it, as well as to the effects of syncope and apocope on the resulting compounds. It is not possible in this paper to discuss the various elements which make up the verbal complex in detail, however, it is necessary to note the following qualities. Firstly, verbs have dependent and independent forms, with dependent forms being used following conjunct particles, including the negative, interrogative and relative particles, the semantically empty verbal particle, "*no*", as well as certain conjunctions. Secondly, Old Irish has compound verbs, comprised of one or more "preverbs" followed by a verbal root. McCone maps how up to five preverbs can precede a verbal root (1997, 90). Thirdly, where the object of the verb is expressed by a pronoun, this pronoun is generally "infixed" between either the initial preverb, or a conjunct particle, and the remainder of the verb, though in certain situations suffixed pronouns are used instead.

The dependent (or "prototonic") forms of compound verbs often look quite different from the independent (or "deuterotonic") forms, as the use of a conjunct particle shifts stress from the second element in the compound to the initial preverb. Hence, negating the compound verb "*dobeir*" ('he gives'), which contains the initial preverb "*do*", results in the prototonic form "*nítabair*" ('he does not give'), where the preverb has become "*ta*". Where a pronoun is infixed into the deuterotonic form it follows the initial preverb, "*do**m**beir*" ('he gives me'), but where it is infixed into the prototonic form it precedes it, "*ní**m**tabair*" ('he does not give me'). This creates a systematic difficulty for tokenisation. If it is desirable to separate the pronoun from the remainder of the verb during tokenisation, this can be achieved in prototonic verb forms without affecting the initial preverb, ("*ní*" + "*m*" + "*tabair*"), but in deuterotonic forms would necessitate separating the initial preverb also, ("*do*" + "*m*" + "*beir*"). The alternative would be to retain "*dombeir*" in its entirety as a single token, and treat the pronoun as if it were verbal morphology. This is the approach taken by POMIC, (see example 4 in Table 1), though hyphenation is used to identify the pronoun. In a more diplomatic edition it would be much more difficult to identify which part of the verb constituted inflection for the verbal object[3].

As can be seen in Table 5, this tokenisation method requires that initial preverbs be separated from the remainders of compound verbs in deuterotonic form, but not in prototonic form. Initial preverbs, therefore, will stand as discrete tokens where verbs occur in deuterotonic form, but will form the stressed anlaut of the verb token itself in prototonic form. Infixed pronouns will always form standalone tokens, as will suffixed pronouns, and all conjunct particles.

The augment, "*ro*"/"*ru*", creates further difficulty. In most cases, it will act as a non-initial preverb, either standing in stressed position, as in "*as**ru**bart*" ('he has said'), or later within the compound, as in "*nito**r**gaítha*" ('he should not defraud him'). In these situations it should be treated as part of the verb token. In rare situations, however, it stands in pretonic position, sometimes even standing between an initial preverb and infixed pronoun, as in "*for**ru**mchennadsa*" ('I have been destroyed', see Thurneysen, 1946, 256). In such cases, it should form its own separate token in the same manner as initial preverbs in deuterotonic forms of verbs ("*for*" + "*ru*" + "*m*" + "*chennad*" + "*sa*").

This tokenisation method is also capable of handling instances of tmesis, where any POS other than an infixed pronoun separates an initial preverb or conjunct particle from the remainder of the verb. A good example of this is "*ad cruth cáin cichither*" ('a beautiful form will be seen'), where both "*cruth*" ('form') and "*cáin*" ('fair/beautiful') are infixed between the preverb, "*ad*", and remainder of the verb, "*cichither*" ('will be seen'). As is demonstrated in Table 4, where tmesis occurs, the initial preverb or conjunct particle, any infixed pronouns, other parts-of-speech preceding the remainder of the verb (such as adjectives and nouns), and the remainder of the verb itself, each form separate tokens from one another.

3.5 Miscellaneous Tokens

Moving away from the verbal complex, a few further tokenisation issues remain. The first regards nasalisation markers (*"m"*/*"ṁ"* and *"n"*/*"ṅ"*), which indicate a phonetic change to the anlaut of a following word. They are generally written as a part of that following word, as in "*is inse **ṅ**duit*" ('it is impossible for you', Wb. 5b28), or "*isdered **ṁ**betho*" ('it is the end of the world', Wb. 10b3), but are also frequently separated from it by spacing, and even enclosed by punctuation (see Bronner, 2016), as in "*a**ṅ** grammatice*" ('the *grammatice*', Sg. 204a8), "*laa **ṁ** brátha*" ('doomsday', Wb. 26a1), and "*lae **.m.** brátho*" (Thurneysen, 1946, 147). In these situations, tokens with internal space characters are permissible, and indeed required by UD treebanks[4]. Therefore, forms like "*ṅ grammatice*", "*ṁ brátha*", and "*.m. brátho*" should be treated as single tokens which contain a space.

Ambiguity may still arise regarding word boundaries where letters have been elided in combinations between clitics and stressed words such as "*i**s**amlid*" (for "*is*" + "*samlid*", 'it is thus'),

[3]Fransen (2020) has demonstrated it may be possible to parse this kind of complex Old Irish verbal morphology using finite state technology, however, no such morphological analyser has yet been made available for general use.

[4]`https://github.com/UniversalDependencies/docs/issues/927`

"*hiṯuilsiu*" (for "*hit*" + "*tuilsiu*", 'in your will'), "*oc̱umtuch*" (for "*oc*" + "*cumtuch*", 'building'), etc. (see Thurneysen, 1946, 91). The rule of thumb adhered to here is that extra letters, which did not occur in the original orthography, should never be supplied during tokenisation. Instead, in accordance with this tokenisation method, the clitic should always lose the letter when separating words, hence, "*isamlid*" = "*i*" + "*samlid*", "*hituilsiu*" = "*hi*" + "*tuilsiu*", and "*ocumtuch*" = "*o*" + "*cumtuch*".

3.6 Abbreviations, Contractions, Symbols and Punctuation

The tokenisation of abbreviations and contractions (where these are not expanded by editors) remains an issue. UD guidelines (Zeman, 2016) suggest that "abbreviations for single words ... are assigned the part of speech of the full form". This is possible for abbreviations like the Tironian *et*, "⁊", which can be simply annotated as a conjunction, as would the full form, "*ocus*" ('and'). It is not possible, however, for abbreviations like "*.i.*" which represent multiple words in Irish, "*ed ón*" ('*id est*'). Instead, such abbreviations should be maintained as discrete tokens, inclusive of any punctuation characters they may have. These can then be POS-tagged as appropriate, for example, "*.i.*" is POS-tagged `ADV` in Old Irish UD treebanks, which matches its treatment in Modern Irish treebanks.

Where a marking or grapheme is used to abbreviate a specific character sequence (such as where "ɔ" stands for "*con*"), these should be treated as if they were letter characters. Where the abbreviated sequence constitutes only a portion of an abbreviated word, the grapheme or marking should form a part of the whole word token. A diplomatic edition may retain the abbreviated token, "*ɔall*", for example, which is equivalent to the normalised form "*Conall*". Similarly, where markings with no set phonetic value, such as suspension strokes, are used to abbreviate some portion of a word, these should form part of the same token as the rest of the word they abbreviate. Again, for example, an abbreviated token like "*ɔchoƀ*", with a suspension stroke above the final letter, *b*, might occur in a diplomatic edition representing the normalised form "*Conchobar*".

The rules outlined in the preceding two paragraphs hold for markings intended to denote abbreviations, even where they include non-letter characters. If, however, a sequence of one or more non-letter characters (such as .·. or .,.,.,) is used in an edition to approximate a manuscript marking which does not denote either an abbreviation, or one or more words (see Groenewegen, 2011), this entire sequence should form a single, discrete token. This token may then be POS-tagged as appropriate. Depending on how it is used, it may be a form of punctuation, or it may be treated as a symbol as in the case of a *signe de renvoi*.

3.7 Applicability to Different Types of Text

While this tokenisation method was designed to be utilised for diplomatically edited Old Irish text it is easily adaptable to texts which have been normalised or otherwise altered by modern editors. For example, in a diplomatic edition "*dombeir*" should be split into three tokens ("*do*" + "*m*" + "*beir*"), however, in another edition an editor may mark the stressed part of the verb using punctuation (hyphenation or a mid-height dot). This should then form its own token and be POS-tagged as punctuation. Hence "*dom·beir*" would be tokenised "*do*" + "*m*" + "·" + "*beir*". As such, this tokenisation method can be applied to any Old or Middle Irish corpus, whether or not it is edited diplomatically. It therefore has the potential to ensure syntactic compatibility between Early Irish text resources in a manner which has not been possible to date.

4 Applications to Old Irish Text

To date the tokenisation method described in this paper has been employed by the online text repository of the Würzburg glosses (Doyle, 2018), as well as by two UD treebanks (Doyle, 2023a,b). In fact, the tokenisation method was developed in tandem with the *Diplomatic St. Gall Glosses* treebank (Doyle, 2023a) and with the *Würzburg Irish Glosses* website (Doyle, 2018) to ensure that it could fulfil the various tokenisation requirements of each corpus. As annotation of these corpora progressed, the tokenisation method was periodically reevaluated and updated as necessary to account for the wide variety of lexical features which occur in these texts.

As the present focus is on tokenising Old Irish text, any more comprehensive discussion of these text resources falls outside the scope of this paper. It is notable, however, that at the time of this writing the entirety of the St. Gall glosses have already been tokenised using the method set out here, including those glosses written in the Ogham script. Therefore, the tokenisation method described in this paper has already been proven to successfully support the consistent separation of word-level tokens throughout a relatively large portion of the surviving body of Old Irish text, and across two writing systems.

5 Future Work

A significant obstacle to the production of large amounts of annotated Old Irish text remains the lack of an automatic tokeniser for the language. The earliest investigation into the viability of such a resource not only demonstrated the considerable difficulty involved in tokenising Old Irish, but also noted that the lack of standardisation between Early Irish text repositories in terms of word separation led to a lack of consistent data with which to train such a model (Doyle et al., 2019). The tokenisation method presented above aims to address this data sparsity by providing a blueprint which could potentially be used to bring discrete text repositories into alignment regarding word boundaries, without needing to alter their raw text content in any way. It is hoped that as more Old Irish text becomes available, which has been tokenised in accordance with the method describe here, it will be possible to train an automatic tokeniser model, and thereby further increase the speed with which Old Irish text can be tokenised and annotated.

6 Conclusion

This paper has demonstrated that the methods by which words are separated in various Old Irish text repositories are inconsistent, making their lexical contents incompatible with one another for the purpose of downstream NLP applications. To address this, a novel tokenisation method has been presented here which can be applied even to diplomatically edited Old Irish text. This removes the impetus to alter the character content of tokens when separating words, a practice which is common in Old Irish text resources.

Before a suitable tokenisation method had been identified for Old Irish, it had not been practicable to standardise the separation of words between Old Irish text resources. The tokenisation method described in this paper has allowed lexical uniformity to exist between resources for the first time. The corpora which have already made use of this tokenisation method are not only the first diplomatically edited Old Irish corpora to have been tokenised, but also the first discrete corpora of Old Irish to share a common word separation method. That it has already been successfully applied to text in three Old Irish resources, including the entirety of the relatively large St. Gall collection of glosses, demonstrates that this new tokenisation method enables consistent tokenisation across a selection of the most challenging scenarios which can result from Old Irish grammar and manuscript orthography.

The importance of word-level compatibility between annotated text resources cannot be understated, though it may be taken for granted in the case of many European languages with more settled spelling and word separation. Particularly where word-level tokens play a role in the application of downstream NLP tasks, any variability between corpora regarding what constitutes a word could potentially skew results. As such, it is envisioned that the tokenisation method presented here will allow for a wider variety of NLP techniques to be applied across the Old Irish texts which already utilise it than would have been possible before. The intention for this paper is that it can act as a reference for those who may wish to tokenise corpora of Early Irish text in the future, and thereby contribute to the lexical standardisation of Early Irish text resources. Ultimately, if this or a comparable tokenisation standard were to become widely adopted by Old Irish text repositories, it is expected that this would not only bolster ongoing linguistic research, but that it could also support new areas of investigation which require more standardised datasets.

Acknowledgements

I would like to express my sincere gratitude to my supervisor, Dr. Clodagh Downey, whose expertise has been invaluable during the course of this research. Without her guidance and keen attention to detail the current work would not be what it is. Any remaining errors and omissions are entirely my own.

This work has been possible thanks to the support of the Science Foundation Ireland (SFI) as part of Grant Number SFI/12/RC/2289_P2 Insight_2, Insight SFI Centre for Data Analytics. This work has also been funded by the University of Galway through the Digital Arts and Humanities Programme, and by the Irish Research Council through the Government of Ireland Postgraduate Scholarship Programme.

References

Bernhard Bauer. 2015. A Dictionary of the Old Irish Priscian Glosses. Accessed: September 12, 2024.

Bernhard Bauer, Rijcklof Hofman, and Pádraic Moran. 2023. St Gall Priscian Glosses, version 2.1. Accessed: September 12, 2024.

Dagmar Bronner. 2016. Nasalierung im Buch von Armagh: Überlegungen zu altirischen Schreibkonventionen. *Zeitschrift für celtische Philologie*, 63(1):29–48.

Oksana Dereza, Theodorus Fransen, and John P. Mccrae. 2023a. Do Not Trust the Experts: How the Lack of Standard Complicates NLP for Historical Irish. In *The Fourth Workshop on Insights from Negative Results in NLP*, pages 82–87, Dubrovnik, Croatia. Association for Computational Linguistics.

Oksana Dereza, Theodorus Fransen, and John P. Mccrae. 2023b. Temporal Domain Adaptation for Historical Irish. In *Tenth Workshop on NLP for Similar Languages, Varieties and Dialects (VarDial 2023)*, Dubrovnik, Croatia. Association for Computational Linguistics.

Adrian Doyle. 2018. Würzburg Irish Glosses. Accessed: September 12, 2024.

Adrian Doyle. 2023a. Diplomatic St. Gall Glosses Treebank. Accessed: September 19, 2024.

Adrian Doyle. 2023b. Diplomatic Würzburg Glosses Treebank. Accessed: September 19, 2024.

Adrian Doyle and John P. McCrae. 2024. Developing a Part-of-speech Tagger for Diplomatically Edited Old Irish Text. In *Proceedings of the Third Workshop on Language Technologies for Historical and Ancient Languages (LT4HALA) @ LREC-COLING-2024*, pages 11–21, Torino, Italia. ELRA and ICCL.

Adrian Doyle, John P. McCrae, and Clodagh Downey. 2019. A Character-Level LSTM Network Model for Tokenizing the Old Irish text of the Würzburg Glosses on the Pauline Epistles. In *Proceedings of the Celtic Language Technology Workshop*, pages 70–79, Dublin, Ireland. European Association for Machine Translation.

e-codices. 2005. e-codices - Virtual Manuscript Library of Switzerland. Accessed: September 12, 2024.

Theodorus Fransen. 2020. Automatic Morphological Analysis and Interlinking of Historical Irish Cognate Verb Forms. In Elliott Lash, Fangzhe Qiu, and David Stifter, editors, *Morphosyntactic Variation in Medieval Celtic Languages. Corpus-Based Approaches*, pages 49–84. De Gruyter Mouton, Berlin.

Aaron Griffith. 2013. A Dictionary of the Old-Irish Glosses. Accessed: September 12, 2024.

Dennis Groenewegen. 2011. Tionscadal na Nod. Accessed: September 21, 2024.

Elliott Lash. 2014a. POMIC Annotation Manual. Manual, The Dublin Institute for Advanced Studies. Accessed: September 15, 2024.

Elliott Lash. 2014b. The Parsed Old and Middle Irish Corpus (POMIC). Version 0.1. Accessed: September 12, 2024.

Kim McCone. 1997. *The Early Irish Verb*, 2 edition. An Sagart, Maynooth.

Beatrice Santorini. 1990. Part-of-Speech Tagging Guidelines for the Penn Treebank Project (3rd Revision). Standard, Department of Computer and Information Science, University of Pennsylvania. Accessed: September 19, 2024.

Beatrice Santorini. 2016. Annotation manual for the Penn Historical Corpora and the York-Helsinki Corpus of Early English Correspondence. Accessed: September 19, 2024.

David Stifter. 2006. *Sengoidelc*. Syracuse University Press, New York.

David Stifter, Bernhard Bauer, Elliott Lash, Fangzhe Qiu, Nora White, Siobhán Barrett, Aaron Griffith, Romanas Bulatovas, Ellen Felici, Francesco abd Ganly, Truc Ha Nguyen, and Lars Nooij. 2021a. Corpus PalaeoHibernicum (CorPH) v1.0. Accessed: September 12, 2024.

David Stifter, Nina Cnockaert-Guillou, Beatrix Färber, Deborah Hayden, Máire Ní Mhaonaigh, Joanna Tucker, and Christopher Guy Yocum. 2021b. Developing a Digital Framework for the Medieval Gaelic World; Project Report. Technical report, Developing a Digital Framework for the Medieval Gaelic World. Accessed: September 23, 2024.

Whitley Stokes and John Strachan, editors. 1901. *Thesaurus Palaeohibernicus*, volume 1. The Dublin Institute for Advanced Studies, Dublin.

Rudolf Thurneysen. 1946. *A Grammar of Old Irish*, 2 edition. The Dublin Institute for Advanced Studies, Dublin.

Gregory Toner, Sharon Arbuthnot, Máire Ní Mhaonaigh, Marie-Luise Theuerkauf, Dagmar Wodtko, Grigory Bondarenko, Maxim Fomin, Thomas Torma, Giuseppina Siriu, Caoimhín Ó Dónaill, and Hilary Lavelle. 2019. eDIL 2019: An Electronic Dictionary of the Irish Language, based on the Contributions to a Dictionary of the Irish Language (Dublin: Royal Irish Academy, 1913-1976). Accessed: September 19, 2024.

Dan Zeman. 2016. UD Guidelines V2. Accessed: September 19, 2024.

Appendix

A Unproblematic Parts-of-speech for Tokenisation of Old Irish

Word Type	Examples	UD POS
Adjectives	*becc, beccaib,* *lugu, lugimen,* *dían, dénithir, déniu,* ***sen** tintúd, is **siniu***	ADJ
Adverbs	*trá, nammá, íarum*	ADV
Anaphoric Pronouns	*do **ṡuidiu**, ol **suide**,* *amal **ṡodain**,* *as beir **side***	PRON
Conjugating Prepositions	*ass, dam, lemm, occaib*	ADP
Deictic Particle	*int **í**, forsna **hí**,* *inna **hí**, a **ní** siu*	PART
Demonstrative Particles	*so, sin*	PART
Nouns	*fer, fir, feraib*	NOUN
Numerals	*tri, téoraib*	NUM
Numeric Particle	***a** óen, **a** cethir, **a** secht*	PART
Vocative Particle	***á** ḟir, **á** chéiliu, **a** rómanu*	PART

Table 2

B Problematic Parts-of-speech for Tokenisation of Old Irish

Word Type	Examples	UD POS
The Article	*in, ind, inna, a,* *la **sin**, la **ssa**, co **ssind**,* *do **nd**, do **naib***	DET
Conjunctions	*ocus, acht, cía, má, ara,* *"cen mitha",* ***ar** ná, **a** nna, **ol** ni, **ma** nip,* ***ce** ni d ḟil, **dia** cairigther,* ***co** naccae, **co** ndom accae,* ***co** ndid tuctis,* ***ci** d, **ci** so, **ma** d, **ma** so*	CCONJ **OR** SCONJ
Emphatic Suffixes	*sa, siu, som,* *mei **sse**, a thu **su**, hé **som***	PRON
Independent Personal Pronouns	*mé, hé, ed, sní,* ***mei** sse, a **thu** su, **hé** som*	PRON
Interrogative Pronouns	*cía, cid, cesí,* ***ci** de, **c** indas on,* ***ci** pad, **cía** bed*	PRON
Possessive Pronouns	*mo, do, a,* ***m** óinur, i **mm** eícndarcus,* *i **t** chóimthecht*	PRON
Prepositions	*a, do, la, oc,* ***a** sind, **do** nd, **la** sin, **oc** ind*	ADP

Table 3

C Tokenisation of the Old Irish Verb and Copula

Word Type	Examples	UD POS
The Verb	*gaibid, biru, caraimm,* *at **tá**, fo **gaib**, as **biur**,* *ní **gaib**, ní **biur**, ní **caraimm**,* *ní **fil**, ní **fagaib**, ní **epur**,* *ní m **fil**, f a **ngaib**, a t **biur**,* *ní s **ngaib**, no b **caraimm**,* *in dam **biur**,* *ad cruth cáin **cichither**,* *no m choimmdiu **cóima***	VERB
The Copula	*am, at, is, ammi, adi, it,* *bid, as, ata,* *níta, ní, nítad,* *nacham, nách, nachib,* *ce **so**, cia **so**, ma **so**,* *ma **d**, ci **d**, co **ndid**,* *a **mtar**, cía **bed**, ci **pad**,* *rop, robbu,* *amal **nonda**, amal **nondad**,* *amal **nondan**, ce **notad***	AUX

Table 4

D Tokenisation of Elements of the Old Irish Verbal Complex

Word Type	Examples	UD POS
The Augment (*ro, ad, com*)	*for **ru** m chennad sa,* *amal **ro** n gab,* *rosechestar, rotoltanaigestar,* *as **rubart**, im **ruidbet**,* *do **rochuirsemmar**,* *ní **roimdibed**, ní **roscríbad**,* *ni **torgaítha**, in **ruchumsan**,* *fo da **rorcenn**,* *ni m **thorgaíth**,* *con **acab**, con **abbong*** *con **ascar**, fris **comorg**,* *do **comrig***	PART **OR** VERB
Conjunct Particles	***ní** léici, **ní** tuit, **ní** fúasna,* ***in** foircnea, **in** naccai,* ***in nád** fail,* ***ní** m léici, **ní** t accai, **ní** tuit,* ***ní** s fúasna, **ní** b ben,* ***nach** am dermainte,* *ar **nach** it rindarpither,* ***in** ndom léici, **in** ndot accai,* ***in** ndid tuit, **in** nda fúasna* ***in** ndob ben*	PART
Infixed Pronouns	*a **tom** chí, a **tot** beir,* *d **a** mbeir, fo **s** ngaib,* *a **t** chí, a **tonn** beir,* *do **b** beir, fo **s** ngaib,* *no **m** chara, no **t** ben,* *n **a** cúalae, ní **s** naccai,* *ní chara, ní **n** ben,* *nách **ib** cúalae, in **da** accai*	PRON
Initial Preverbs	**DEUTEROTONIC** ***ad** cí, **do** beir, **fo** gaib,* ***du** airṅgir,* ***a** tot chí, **d** a beir,* ***fo** m gaib, **do** b airṅgir,* **PROTOTONIC** *ní **accai**, ní **tabair**, ní **fagaib**,* *ní **tairngir**,* *ní t **accai**, ní **tabair**,* *ní m **fagaib**, ní b **tairngir***	PART **OR** VERB
Relative Particle	*ar **a**, di **a**, hu **a**, la **sa**, oc **a***	PART
Suffixed Pronouns	*beirth **i**, léicsi **us**, guidm **it***	PRON
Verbal Particle (*no/nu*)	***no** bed, **no** berinn,* ***no** léicthea, **no** marbthae,* ***no** m chara, **n** a cara,* ***no** b cara, **no** da deligedar,* ***no** nda failsigetar,* *ce **nu** d sluindi*	PART

Table 5

Synthesising a Corpus of Gaelic Traditional Narrative with Cross-Lingual Text Expansion

William Lamb[1], Dongge Han[1,2], Ondřej Klejch[1], Beatrice Alex[1], Peter Bell[1]

[1]University of Edinburgh, [2]Microsoft Corporation
Correspondence: w.lamb@ed.ac.uk

Abstract

Advances in large language modelling have disproportionately benefited high-resource languages due to their vastly greater training data reserves. This paper proposes a novel cross-lingual text expansion (XLTE) technique using multilingual large language models (MLLMs) to mitigate data sparsity in low-resource languages. We apply XLTE to the domain of traditional Scottish Gaelic storytelling to generate a training corpus suitable for language modelling, for example as part of an automatic speech recognition system. The effectiveness of this technique is demonstrated using OpenAI's GPT-4o, with supervised fine-tuning (SFT) providing decreased neologism rates and a 57.2% reduction in perplexity over the baseline model. Despite these promising results, qualitative analyses reveal important stylistic divergences between synthesised and genuine data. Nevertheless, XLTE offers a promising, scalable method for synthesising training sets in other languages and domains, opening avenues for further improvements in low-resource language modelling.

1 Introduction

Recent breakthroughs in natural language processing (NLP), particularly the development of large language models (LLMs), have principally benefited well-resourced languages like English and Spanish. Most of the world's languages remain marginalised, however, due to a lack of suitable training data (Magueresse et al., 2020; Joshi et al., 2020). Training even a GPT-2-scale LLM, for example, requires roughly 10B tokens of text.[1] This far exceeds the extant corpus of most low-resource languages (LRLs). While many high-resource languages (HRLs) can exploit web-scale datasets, languages like Gaelic – spoken by 69,701 individuals in Scotland (National Records of Scotland, 2022) – can offer only a minute fraction of such data.

A promising solution to the sparsity problem facing LRLs is coupling synthetic text generation with cross-lingual transfer (Chen et al., 2019). Multilingual large language models (MLLMs) like BLOOM (Scao et al., 2022), GPT (Radford et al., 2018) and LLaMA (Dubey et al., 2024) are trained on manifold languages, enabling them to transfer knowledge from high-resource languages to tasks involving LRLs. What if we could harness these cross-lingual capacities to produce useful training data for LRLs, for instance towards language modelling? In other words, could we prompt a MLLM to generate a training corpus in a LRL?

The digital text available for Gaelic is approximately 150M tokens but the language is better-resourced for audio data. This is due, in part, to the thousands of hours of ethnographic recordings made of Gaelic speakers in the mid-20th century. If we could reliably transcribe these audio data, we could substantially augment the language's textual resources. A key objective of ongoing work is to automatically transcribe recordings of traditional narrative, many of which are hosted on the online portal Tobar an Dualchais / Kist o Riches.[2] About 1M words of high-quality narrative text exist from earlier digitisation and recognition efforts (Sinclair et al., 2022; Meaney et al., 2024), but a much larger corpus is needed to improve automatic speech recognition (ASR) for this domain (Evans et al., 2022).

We hypothesise that we can increase our narrative training data by deploying a novel *cross-lingual text expansion* (XLTE) method. Text expansion is converting a short text into a longer one (Dong et al., 2022). XLTE couples expansion with translation: it involves prompting a MLLM with a summary in one language to generate an extended

[1]Radford et al., 2018 used 40GB of text to train GPT-2, which amounts to about 10B tokens.

[2]`https://www.tobarandualchais.co.uk`

Proceedings of the 5th Celtic Language Technology Workshop (CLTW 5), pages 12–26
Abu Dhabi, UAE (Online), January 20, 2025

text in another language. For our use-case, we fine-tune a MLLM using transcriptions of oral Gaelic narratives paired with their English summaries. We then generate a synthetic corpus of narrative using a held out set of English summaries.[3] We hypothesise that fine-tuning a MLLM for this task will improve results over generating using a baseline model. We use OpenAI's GPT-4o model (OpenAI, 2024; Islam and Moushi, 2024)[4] but expect that XLTE could be extended to other MLLMs with API access and fine-tuning capabilities, such as Claude (Anthropic, 2024) or LLaMA, provided they offer similar coverage for a target LRL.

To explore our hypotheses, we adopt the following research questions:

1. What benefits, if any, does supervised fine-tuning (SFT) offer over the baseline GPT model for using XLTE to generate a synthetic corpus of Gaelic traditional narrative?

2. How do texts generated using XLTE compare with genuine ones across intrinsic evaluation metrics?

3. What stylistic differences, if any, can be detected between our synthetic and genuine narrative texts?

The organisation of the remaining paper is as follows: §2 provides background information and surveys relevant literature; §3 describes our datasets and methodology; §4 presents and discusses our results and, finally, §5 offers concluding remarks and future research possibilities.

2 Background and Related Work

2.1 Large Language Models (LLMs)

Progress in NLP has been catalysed by the emergence of large language models, especially the variety known as Generative Pre-trained Transformers (GPTs). During pre-training, these models use self-attention (Vaswani et al., 2017) within a next-token prediction task, inducing the relative importance of each token in an input stream to every other token (Raiaan et al., 2024). Through this process, they can compress a vast input corpus (e.g. all of the Internet's text) into a high-dimensional, context-cognisant representation of a language's vocabulary, linguistic features and associated 'world-knowledge' (Zhao et al., 2023).

For many applications, a pre-trained base-model can be improved through additional training known as *supervised fine-tuning* (SFT). SFT involves updating some of the model's parameters using labelled data, and biasing the model to produce more accurate classification or generation results given a particular prompt (e.g. 'Expand the given summary into a longer traditional narrative in Scottish Gaelic') and supervised dataset (Chen et al., 2024; Mosbach et al., 2023; Qin et al., 2022). SFT is quicker and requires fewer resources than training a model from scratch but delivers improved performance for many applications (Zhao et al., 2023). In the present study, we investigate whether SFT enhances the capabilities of GPT-4o to generate Gaelic traditional narrative texts over using the base model. In general, this study aligns with a body of NLP research that examines augmenting or creating domain-specific training data where little to none exist.

2.2 LLM-based Synthetic Text Generation

Using LLMs to synthesise training corpora and supervised data is a growing research area across multiple domains (see Ding et al., 2024, Guo and Chen, 2024 and Sufi, 2024 for recent reviews). Common use-cases include generating labelled medical data (Falis et al., 2024), plausible questionnaire responses (Hämäläinen et al., 2023), multi-turn dialogue data (Xu et al., 2023) and low-resource machine translation data (Lucas et al., 2024; Hong et al., 2024). Notably, one study on another LRL (Arabic) demonstrated that LLMs built on GPT-2-generated text performed comparably to ones built using the outputs of optical character recognition (OCR) and ASR for a range of natural language understanding tasks (Alcoba Inciarte et al., 2024). Evidence has emerged that training LLMs iteratively on synthetic text leads to diminished linguistic diversity and model collapse (Guo and Chen, 2024; Dohmatob et al., 2024; Shumailov et al., 2024). Nevertheless, this is not a concern for the present study given that we deploy first-generation synthesised data only; no iteration is involved.

Salient to our present aims, several recent papers have investigated how well LLMs produce long-form texts, such as fiction and storytelling (Yang et al., 2022; Xie and Riedl, 2024; Tian et al., 2024;

[3] Performance tends to be better when using English prompts versus ones in the target language (Bareiß et al., 2024)).

[4] OpenAI approached us in June 2023 as part of an initiative to collaborate with low-resource speech communities.

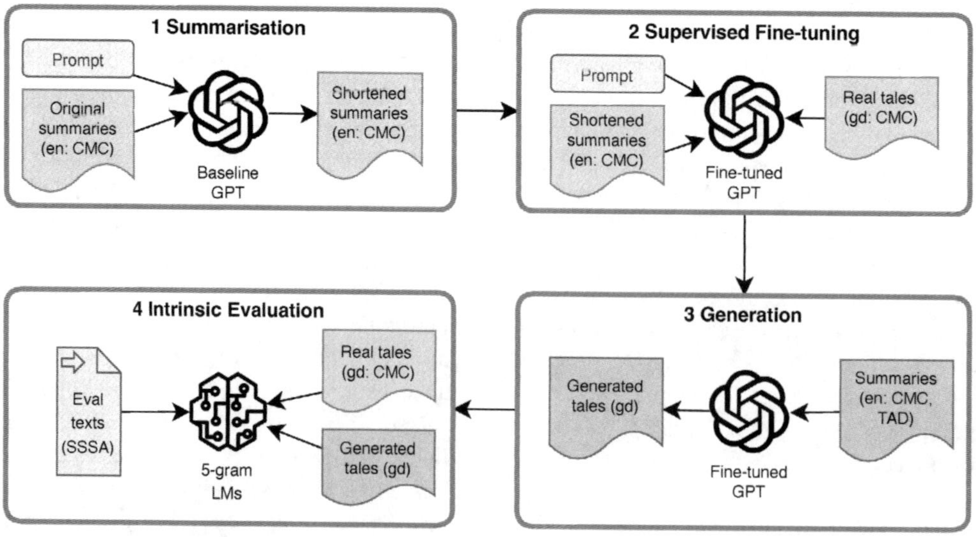

Figure 1: Training and evaluation pipeline. The summarisation prompt was 'Summarise the given text in 6 to 7 sentences'. The supervised fine-tuning and generation prompt was 'You will receive a summary in English. Expand the summary into a longer traditional narrative in Scottish Gaelic'. The datasets in Table 1 map to the pipeline's steps as: Tr (1, 2); Tr-100 (1, 2, 4); Val (1, 2); Gen (3); Eval (4). Language key: en 'English'; gd 'Gaelic'.

Qi et al., 2024). In general, they find that current models like GPT-4o can produce coherent narratives up to about 2,000 words in English, but that text quality degrades in step with length after this point (Que et al., 2024). It is worth noting that transcriptions of Gaelic traditional narrative often exceed this word count (see Table 2). Additionally, MLLMs have been shown to have quality issues when generating synthetic text in LRLs (Robinson et al., 2023; Lai et al., 2023; Nguyen et al., 2023). Therefore, we expect to see more pronounced quality degradation in Gaelic long-form, synthetic texts due to weaker representations in pre-training corpora. To our knowledge, however, the area of LLM-based long-form text generation for LRLs remains unstudied.

2.3 Cross-lingual Transfer with MLLMs

An interesting property of MLLMs is their ability to share information between languages, known as *cross-lingual transfer*. To date, cross-lingual summarisation research involving MLLMs has focused on simultaneous translation and summarisation (see Wang et al., 2022). Here, instead, we attempt to share the knowledge encoded in GPT-4o's English-based representations with Gaelic by expanding a summary in the former to a full text in the latter.

The quality of cross-lingual transfer between two languages depends on the degree of alignment between their feature spaces (Schmidt et al., 2022). Given the linguistic distance between Gaelic and English, and the presumed sparse Gaelic data in GPT-4o's pre-training corpus, one might expect our generation quality to be quite low. Yet, in theory, we also may be able to leverage GPT-4o's representations of a related and better-resourced Celtic language for our task, Irish. Positive transfer between higher-resource and lower-resource languages comes partially from the overlap in shared word-piece tokens (Conneau et al., 2020; Maguer-esse et al., 2020). Although Irish and Gaelic have somewhat distinct orthographies and grammar, they share a large proportion of lemmas (e.g. Irish *ballaí* 'walls' → *balla* 'wall'; Gaelic *ballachan* 'walls' → *balla* 'wall'). The implicit alignment between Irish and Gaelic sub-words, therefore, may benefit our task.

3 Datasets

To increase the available training data for Gaelic traditional narrative, we propose using XLTE, fine-tuning GPT-4o to produce long Gaelic narratives when prompted with an English summary of a traditional tale. Table 1 lists the six datasets used for this study and Figure 1 summarises the processing pipeline at a glance (see §4 for further details).

The 'CMC' data came from an orthographically standardised subset of the Calum Maclean Collection, an online corpus of Gaelic folktales.[5] The data contain transcriptions of Gaelic folktales paired with manually-produced English summaries and were split into training ('Tr'), validation ('Val') and generation ('Gen') sets using a 80:10:10 ratio. The Tr and Val sets were used during supervised fine-tuning (Step 2 in Fig 1). The English summaries of the CMC Gen and the TAD Gen sets provided generation stimuli (Step 3 in Fig 1). We also created a CMC training set of the 100 longest tales ('Tr-100'), to explore whether models fine-tuned on this set would produce longer, higher-quality outputs. As can be seen in Table 2, the word count distributions of the Tr sets are right-skewed; the median is a better measure of central tendency than the mean here.

The evaluation set ('Eval') comprised 158 Gaelic oral narrative texts from the Tale Archive of the School of Scottish Studies Archives (SSSA: see Sinclair et al., 2022). We used this as a reference set for computing the perplexity of various downstream n-gram LMs (see §4.4). Finally, a test set of 1,857 English summaries ('TAD') was used to prompt our best-performing fine-tuned model and assess XLTE for this use-case at scale. The TAD dataset comprised manual summaries of Gaelic folktales produced for the Tobar an Dualchais / Kist o Riches project[6] and is orthogonal to the CMC Gen set.

Source	Lang	Set	N	Words-gd
CMC	en/gd	Tr	384	276,958
CMC	en/gd	Tr-100	100	203,447
CMC	en/gd	Val	48	33,989
CMC	en	Gen	49	91,982
SSSA	gd	Eval	158	729,867
TAD	en	Gen	1,857	N/A

Table 1: Dataset statistics (gd: Gaelic; en: English)

4 Methodology

The processing pipeline, visualised in Figure 1, consists of four main steps. In Step 1 ('Summarisation'), we prompt the baseline GPT-4o model to condense the human-generated English summary for each narrative in the training set. This step ensures consistency in summary length between the training and generation sets (see Table 1) and creates the paired data necessary for supervised fine-tuning (SFT). Step 2 ('Supervised Fine-Tuning') involves adapting the GPT-4o model to produce a naturalistic Gaelic narrative when given a plausible English summary. In Step 3 ('Generation'), we synthesise a corpus of Gaelic narratives using the fine-tuned model, prompting it with authentic English summaries from held-out generation sets. Finally, in Step 4 ('Intrinsic Evaluation'), we construct an n-gram language model (LM) from both the generated and genuine texts and evaluate their predictive accuracy on a held-out evaluation set. The following subsections provide further details on this pipeline.

Dataset	Mean	Median	St Dev
Tr	807.9	336	1747.6
Tr-100	2811.9	1652	3099.6

Table 2: Word count statistics of CMC training sets

4.1 Summarisation

While the TAD English summaries were 6.4 sentences and 78.8 words long on average, the original CMC English summaries were 14.2 sentences and 268.7 words long. We prompted the baseline GPT-4o model to condense the CMC summaries and equalise them with the TAD summaries' average length. To accomplish this, we used the *system message* ('prompt'), 'Summarise the given text in 6 to 7 sentences', and the following hyperparameter settings: n = 1, temperature = 1; top-p = 0.85; presence-penalty = 0.2; frequency-penalty = 0 and max-tokens = 250.

4.2 Supervised Fine-tuning

We assessed whether SFT would benefit this use-case or if the baseline GPT-4o model was sufficient. The SFT prompt was the same as that used for generation (Step 3): 'You will receive a summary in English. Expand the summary into a longer traditional narrative in Scottish Gaelic'. After experimentation with hyperparameters, we fine-tuned for 3 epochs with a batch size of 1 and a learning rate multiplier of 2. As is standard, we monitored loss on both the training set and validation set to mitigate the risk of over-fitting.

[5] https://www.calum-maclean-project.celtscot.ed.ac.uk/home/

[6] https://www.tobarandualchais.co.uk. Note that a word count is not listed for the TAD source in Table 1 given that it consists of English summaries only; it contains no Gaelic text.

4.3 Generation

During generation, we prompted the models to expand the English summaries to longer Gaelic texts using the same system message as in the SFT step (see §4.2). After initial testing, we determined that the following hyperparameters achieve useful textual diversity, attenuate repetition and produce longer outputs: n = 1, temperature = 1; top-p = 0.5; presence-penalty = 0.3; frequency-penalty = 0.2 and max-tokens = 1000.

4.4 Evaluation Procedures

We deploy the following intrinsic evaluation metrics to assess the quality and performance of the generated texts:

- *mean word count* (MWC), which measures a GPT model's productivity; all things being equal, higher is preferred, due to lower generation costs and processing time
- *mean English to Gaelic ratio* (en:gd), a measure of code-switching levels, where lower is generally better;[7]
- *neologisms per total word count* (Neo), an estimation of hallucinated and nonce words, where lower is better;
- *perplexity* (PPL), which indicates the extent to which a LM predicts a textual input, where lower is better.

The English to Gaelic ratio is computed by calculating how many tokens in a given text occur in a large English dictionary, divided by how many occur in a large Gaelic dictionary. Tokens found in neither dictionary are considered neologisms[8] – hallucinated and otherwise out-of-dictionary tokens, many of which appear to be a by-product of Byte Pair Encoding (BPE) (Iwamoto and Kanayama, 2024). Perplexity measures the predictive accuracy of a LM against a reference text. Mathematically, it is the inverse of the geometric mean of the probabilities that a LM assigns to a text (Brown et al., 1992). Although perplexity is a commonly-deployed proxy for 'output quality', we acknowledge that it has an uneven relationship with human annotator scores (Stureborg et al., 2024). Additionally, it can be affected by superficial features such as text length (Meister and Cotterell, 2021) and punctuation (Wang et al., 2023).

To calculate perplexity on our texts, we lowercase and normalise them and then train a BPE tokeniser (Gage, 1994; Sennrich et al., 2016) on the full Gaelic narrative corpus, tokenising all input texts. Next, we train a 5-gram LM for the generated text with modified Kneser-Ney smoothing and no pruning, using the KenLM package (Heafield et al., 2013). We also train a LM using genuine narratives from the Tr-100 training set for comparison. As mentioned in §3, perplexity is calculated against the Eval set, comprising the SSSA texts.

5 Results and Discussion

In this section, we provide and discuss our experimental results. To recapitulate, our aim is to use XLTE to generate a synthetic corpus of Gaelic traditional narrative that can be used for downstream NLP tasks, such as training an external LM for an ASR system. Although this application is outwith the present scope, it will be examined in future research.[9]

5.1 Intrinsic Evaluation

We fine-tuned GPT-4o on the Tr (n=384) and Tr-100 (n=100) training sets (see Table 1) using the hyperparameter settings described in §4.2. We then trained n-gram language models on 48 examples of real training data (Train), data generated with the baseline GPT-4o model (4o-base) and the fine-tuned models (FT-100, FT-384). As shown in Table 3, the LMs associated with the fine-tuned models showed reduced perplexity scores on the Eval set, which indicates better predictive accuracy. Specifically, the LM associated with FT-100 achieved a PPL of 258.4, and FT-384 achieved 274.2, compared to the much higher PPL of 604.3 for the LM built from the baseline GPT-4o model's output. We observe that the FT-100 LM, which was trained upon the 100 longest narratives in the training set, achieved a slightly lower PPL value than the model trained on the full training set (FT-384), despite its smaller size. We expect that this occurred given that the FT-100 model generated longer texts on

[7]One could argue that it should resemble that of genuine narratives.

[8]We manually annotated a random sample of 100 automatically identified 'neologisms' and found 68% nonce words and compounds, 13% well-formed Gaelic compounds, 8% misspelled Gaelic words, 6% plausible dialectal variants, 3% Gaelic names and 2% English names.

[9]ASR for traditional narrative almost certainly will benefit from a language model built from a large, diverse dataset. Realistically, synthetic text from the target domain – if useful – would comprise only part of it.

average than the FT-384 model and had a slightly reduced neologism ratio.

Overall, the fine-tuned models are more productive than the baseline model, and have fewer English words and neologisms. These results suggest that fine-tuning, even on relatively small datasets, offers improvements in language modelling for this low-resource context. At the same time – and unsurprisingly – a LM built using the fine-tuning training data itself (i.e. the genuine transcriptions of Gaelic narrative in CMC) achieves a lower PPL still.[10] Thus, a model built directly on real data is likely to have a stronger grasp of the linguistic structures and discourse patterns inherent in the original texts.

Model	PPL	MWC	en:gd	Neo
FT-100	**258.4**	361.4	0.003	0.013
FT-384	274.2	330.5	0.003	0.014
4o-base	604.3	284.0	0.005	0.023
Train	140.2	630.3	0.007	0.007

Table 3: Intrinsic evaluation metrics for 48 generated (FT-100, FT-384 and 4o-base) and real narratives (Train). The results show improved performance of fine-tuned models over GPT-4o baseline on perplexity (PPL), mean word count (MWC), English to Gaelic ratio (en:gd) and neologism to total word count ratio (Neo). Metrics for the training set (Train) are provided for comparison.

To estimate the downstream benefits from using a larger amount of synthetic text, we use the FT-100 model to generate 1857 narratives (487,943 words) from the Gen set summaries (see §3) and concatenate these outputs with the original Tr-100 narrative texts. The results (see Table 4) indicate that scaling up the generated data improves the predictive power of the LMs built from them. Specifically, the PPL associated with a LM built using outputs derived from the Gen set summaries is lower (150.3) than that built using 48 outputs generated from the Tr-100 set summaries (258.4: see Table 3). Nevertheless, the LM built from authentic text achieves a superior PPL of 93.9, outperforming those built from generated data alone (PPL = 150.3) or concatenated real and generated data (PPL = 95.7). In comparison, we find that concatenating real and generated data enhances language models for the Gaelic news script domain (to be detailed in a future paper). To achieve a similar result in the narrative domain, we may need to increase the diversity of the SFT training data.[11]

Model	PPL	MWC	en:gd	Neo
Tr-100	**93.9**	1966.2	0.006	0.008
Gen	150.3	256.4	0.003	0.010
Concat	95.7	343.9	0.004	0.012

Table 4: Intrinsic evaluation metrics for the FT-100 training set (Tr-100, n=100), a large set of narratives generated with the FT-100 model (Gen, n=1857) and concatenated real and generated data (Concat, n=1957).

In sum, for this language, this MLLM and this use-case, one can generate a large synthetic training corpus with minimal effort and resources. Moreover, conducting XLTE with a fine-tuned GPT-4o model offers a clear performance boost over using the base model. The quality of the synthesised corpus, however, does not match human-produced data (cf. Alcoba Inciarte et al., 2024). This accords with research showing that MLLMs struggle to generate high quality output for LRLs (Robinson et al., 2023; Lai et al., 2023; Nguyen et al., 2023). Improvements may come from fine-tuning with larger training sets, further training epochs or increased learning rates. Nonetheless, it is possible that GPT-4o is under-resourced for Gaelic traditional narrative. Greater utility may come from training a LM on concatenated authentic and synthesised data when targeting domains that are better represented in GPT-4o's training data.

5.2 Stylistic Differences

To better understand divergences between the synthetic and genuine data for this use-case, we compared them for features that have been identified in previous research as being characteristic of Gaelic narrative, and spontaneous speech more broadly (Lamb, 2008). These are: 1) opening and closing formulas; 2) the narrative past-tense verb *arsa* 'quoth', used for direct quotation and 3) cosubordination. These features are likely amongst those implicit in perplexity differences although they are difficult to isolate programmatically. Here, we provide preliminary notes on the distributional and qualitative differences of these features in the datasets. We also briefly compare one synthetic narrative with its genuine counterpart.

[10] The longer average word count of the genuine narratives (630.3) likely accounts for some of the lower perplexity value; perplexity tends to negatively correlate with text length (Meister and Cotterell, 2021; Wang et al., 2023).

[11] As one reviewer points out, the better results for the news domain may come from the Gaelic pre-training corpus comprising mostly written text versus transcriptions of speech.

5.2.1 Opening and closing formulas

Traditional Gaelic storytellers often employ *formulas* in tales – stock phrases with myriad functions. The formula *bha siud ann (roimhe)* 'that was there (before)' is a common opening phrase and broadly equivalent to 'once upon a time' in English. While 17% of genuine tales from the Tr-100 set evince this formula, it occurs in none of the 1,857 generated tales from the Gen set. On the other hand, 18% of the generated tales begin with a more general variant, *bha* [noun phrase] *ann*, such as *bha tighearna ann roimhe* 'there was once a laird'. In comparison, only 5% of genuine tales have this variant. We believe that this finding can be explained by the fact that the phrase *bha* [NP] *ann* is generic and well-represented in GPT-4o's Gaelic pre-training corpus; it occurs in the language in other contexts. On the other hand, the prevalence of the more narrative-specific opening in the FT-100 training data was not high enough to induce the fine-tuned model to generate it.

Similarly, a common closing formula of Gaelic narratives is *agus dhealaich mi riutha* 'and I departed from them', which functions like the English phrase 'and they lived happily for ever after'. While this occurs in 26% of genuine tales, it does not appear in a single generated tale.

Taken together, these findings suggest that our fine-tuning conditions were not sufficient for GPT-4o to learn specific opening and closing formulas for Gaelic narrative. Although the model did learn a more general opening formula, it deployed it more frequently than would be expected in a genuine corpus. The complete lack of closing formulas may be a sign of attention decay (Li et al., 2024) during the fine-tuning process. Here, the model attends more to tokens or words that appear earlier in a sequence and less on tokens that appear later. Autoregressive LLMs generate text by iteratively predicting each token based on a probability distribution conditioned upon the input prompt and all previously-generated tokens. Thus, the model's prediction at each step relies on the context formed by the tokens generated so far. With increased context sizes, such as posed by longer narratives, performance can suffer. During generation, the lack of closing formulas may also be a sign of excessive weight on the local context at the detriment of the global context, a known problem with GPT models (Zhang et al., 2023). Based upon these results, it may be fruitful in the future to investigate diverging text quality and coherence in the heads and tails of long outputs.

5.2.2 Narrative direct-quotation verb

The defective verb *arsa/ars* 'quoth, said', or its variant *orsa/ors*, is a common feature of the storytelling register, where it is used to report direct speech. It often occurs in the register preferentially to another, more generic verb *thuirt* 'said', particularly in long stretches of dialogue. While the frequency for *arsa* is 37.6 per 1k words in the genuine texts, it is less than half that (16.4) in the synthetic texts. It is possible that an enhanced fine-tuning regimen, as discussed in §5.1, might encourage the model to adapt more closely to this and other stylistic features of the register.

5.2.3 Cosubordination

Cosubordination is a linguistic construction found in Gaelic and certain other languages (Van Valin and LaPolla, 1997) whereby a finite independent clause is coordinated with a non-finite dependent clause: e.g. *rinn e e agus iad nan cadal* 'He did it while [lit. and] they were asleep'. Cosubordination has been found to be closely associated with narrative registers (Lamb, 2008).

Using regular expressions, we searched for a type of cosubordination that is signposted by the occurrence of *agus* 'and' and a pronoun. In genuine narrative texts, this construction appeared 0.8 times per 1k words, but in synthetic texts, it appeared at 1/4 this rate: only 0.2 times per 1k words. Again, by strengthening the fine-tuning procedure – through increased stimuli or hyperparameter modification, or both – it may be possible to increase its appearance in synthetic texts. At the same time, if cosubordination and other constructions typical of traditional narrative are uncommon in pre-training data, it may be impossible to enhance the idiomaticity of synthetic text for this use-case beyond a certain margin. Of course, this may or not be detrimental to a particular application. For instance, if the synthetic text is used to train an n-gram LM, positive impacts on downstream tasks (e.g. ASR) may be possible even if the data are not fully concordant with the target domain.

5.2.4 Comparison of a synthetic and genuine narrative text

To further probe the fine-tuned model's output, we compared a synthetic text generated from one summary stimulus with a transcription of the original

Gaelic audio. These texts are available in Appendix A.[12]

The clearest difference between the synthetic and authentic text is that the former is shorter: its word count is 172, in contrast to 384 for the genuine text. Overall, we found generated text lengths somewhat labile; word counts for ten repeated generations in OpenAI's playground – using this summary and the hyperparameters stated in §5.1 – ranged from 90 to 561, with a mean of 196.

To expand a summary, the model must deploy its ingested knowledge to fill in the gaps logically. It is therefore useful to consider what the model adds to the synthetic text beyond the information that the summary provides. In this synthetic text example, the key place-name has mutated from Gerinish (*Geirinis*) to Garrynomonie (*Gearraidh na Mònadh*), another township in South Uist. The model infers from the label 'spinsters' that the women are socially isolated or awkward. Although this is a somewhat mild example of bias, it underlines the well-established tendency of LLMs to perpetuate negative stereotypes against women and older individuals (Zhao et al., 2024; Kamruzzaman et al., 2024; O'Connor and Liu, 2024).

Hallucination is well-known problem of LLM generation, whereby outputs are erroneous, contradictory or cannot be fact-checked (Ji et al., 2023). As introduced in §4.4, a sub-type of hallucination that affects our synthetic texts is LLM neologism, when a LLM outputs a word that cannot be found in a language's accepted lexicon (Iwamoto and Kanayama, 2024). Two neologisms occur in the synthetic output presented in Appendix A: *maighstir-sgioblaid* [recte *sgiobair*], which appears for 'captain', and *shùisg*, which is used for 'spit out' or 'vomit'. The first case is a compound of real and nonce elements. The modifier *maighstir* 'master' is a genuine word. The head noun, *sgioblaid*, appears to graft the element *sgiob-*, which is used in the words *sgioba* 'team' and *sgiobair* 'skipper', with *-laid*, an opaque ending that occurs in several real words (e.g. *trioblaid* 'trouble'). Regarding the second case, bodily functions in Gaelic are normally verbalised periphrastically (Lamb, 2024), that is using a generic verb (e.g. *dèan* 'do') along with the salient noun (e.g. *smugaid* 'spittle' $\rightarrow$ *dèan smugaid* 'spit' [lit. *make spit*]). Several natural Gaelic nouns meaning 'spit' begin with *s-*, but few verbs do. Additionally, no words with this connotation, to our knowledge, end in *-ùisg*. Yet the neologism *shùisg* 'spat, vomit' is perfectly understandable and even onomatopoeic. Although byte pair encoding is the transparent culprit for the first example, the second is more difficult to explain.

Another surprising element in the synthetic output is the appearance of gender agreement between pronouns and inanimate nouns: *brot* ('broth, soup', a masculine noun) maps correctly to *e* (a masculine pronoun) and *feòil* ('meat', a feminine noun) maps to *i* (a feminine pronoun). This type of agreement is waning in the spoken language. Its presence here suggests that, during pre-training, GPT-4o implicitly induced nominal gender as part of the embedding process and that MLLMs can share gender representations between higher- and lower-resource languages (Gonen et al., 2022). Future research could examine whether the publicly-available digital corpus for Gaelic is sufficient for MLLMs to reliably embed nominal gender representations, or if other related (e.g. Irish) and unrelated (e.g. French) languages produce a shared subspace for grammatical gender.

Turning to the genuine narrative example in Appendix A, we observe greater contextualisation and linguistic fluency, as expected from authentic storytelling. Specifically, the women are named, a historical context is provided (e.g. it happened twenty-three years ago and WWII rationing was in effect) and the location is given more precisely (i.e. the ship sunk at the Strait of Eriskay). In terms of lexis, the English word 'soup' is used instead of the less common Gaelic word *brot* 'broth, soup'. Also, the more charged label *Pàpanach* 'papist' is deployed instead of the more neutral *Caitligeach* 'Catholic', which appears in the synthetic text. Although the connotations of *Pàpanach* are milder in Gaelic than those of 'papist' in English, it would be unlikely to appear in formal Gaelic discourse. Although some MLLMs now offer basic support for LRLs like Gaelic, identifying and mitigating bias in these languages presents unique challenges due to toxicity and sparsity in training data, and cultural nuances. While addressing biases in HRLs is an active research area (Ferrara, 2023), additional work is needed to gauge how well current debiasing methods work for LRLs and how well they preserve linguistic and cultural diversity.

[12] We also provide a text generated with the baseline GPT-4o model for transparency. The baseline model's output is longer than that of the fine-tuned model, but it resembles a 19th century written homily more than a modern, vernacular folktale.

6 Conclusions

This study introduces cross-lingual text expansion (XLTE) as a scalable, LLM-driven method for mitigating data sparsity in low-resource languages and domains. By fine-tuning GPT-4o to expand English summaries into Gaelic narratives, we generated a substantial synthetic corpus that shows promise for improving language models. Our results demonstrate that supervised fine-tuning enhances performance over baseline GPT models, resulting in substantial reductions in perplexity and neologism. One surprising element found in synthetic texts was the appearance of gender-marked pronominal reference, which is fading from spontaneous spoken Gaelic. Nevertheless, qualitative analysis revealed stylistic discrepancies between synthetic and authentic narratives, particularly in terms of diminished formulaic language, narrative-specific verbs and cosubordination.

Future research should aim to narrow these stylistic gaps by improving the fine-tuning processes, for example by using more diverse, domain-specific training data and conducting further hyperparameter optimisation. One useful avenue would be to examine the relationship between top-p and hallucination (cf. Massarelli et al., 2020). Another would be to examine the effects of different prompts, such as explicitly declaring the desired word count. Given the limitations of working with a proprietary model, adapting the study to an open MLLM such as Meta's LLaMA (Etxaniz et al., 2024) would produce valuable insights. It also would be interesting to assess whether XLTE is more successful for domains that are better represented in pre-training corpora, such as news reportage. To conclude, we expect that XLTE is applicable to other domains and low-resource languages and has the potential to advance language modelling capabilities and downstream language technologies across diverse use-cases.

Limitations

The key limitation of this work is that it deploys a closed, proprietary large language model, GPT-4o. Beyond the basic details in OpenAI, 2024, OpenAI have not published information on GPT-4o's architecture, training data or fine-tuning procedures. This hinders the transparency and replicability of our study. For instance, we are unable to detect or remedy potential biases in the Gaelic training data or evaluate the model directly.

Acknowledgments

This work has benefited from the support of the Scottish Government (Grant name: 'Ecosystem for Interactive Speech Technologies') and the Arts and Humanities Research Council and Irish Research Council (Grant name: 'Decoding Hidden Heritages'; Grant numbers AH/W001934/1 and IRC/W001934/1). Thank you to the National Folklore Collection (University College Dublin) for permission to use data from the Calum Maclean Project, and to Tobar an Dualchais / Kist o Riches for providing access to the English and Gaelic summary data. Many thanks to Cailean Gordon for checking the Gaelic transcription and to Colin Jarvis of OpenAI for providing training credits and model access. Finally, we are grateful to the three anonymous reviewers for their constructive comments and advice.

Statement on Ethics

Institutional ethical review for this research was instigated on 2 March 2023 and granted on 13 March 2023 by the Ethics Officer of the host institution. Although no substantial risks are associated with this work, the authors acknowledge the environmental impact associated with pre-training large language models and, to a lesser extent, fine-tuning and generating from them. As a proprietary model was used for this study, it is impossible to provide an accurate measure of the carbon emissions associated with it at this time.

References

Alcides Alcoba Inciarte, Sang Yun Kwon, El Moatez Billah Nagoudi, and Muhammad Abdul-Mageed. 2024. On the utility of pretraining language models on synthetic data. In *Proceedings of The Second Arabic Natural Language Processing Conference*, pages 265–282, Bangkok, Thailand. Association for Computational Linguistics.

Anthropic. 2024. Claude 3 model card. Accessed: 2024-10-08.

Patrick Bareiß, Roman Klinger, and Jeremy Barnes. 2024. English prompts are better for NLI-based zero-shot emotion classification than target-language prompts. In *Companion Proceedings of the ACM on Web Conference 2024*, pages 1318–1326.

Peter Brown, Della Pietra, Vincent J, Peter V Desouza, Jennifer C Lai, and Robert L Mercer. 1992. Class-based n-gram models of natural language. *Computational Linguistics*, 18(4):467–480.

Xilun Chen, Ahmed Hassan Awadallah, Hany Hassan, Wei Wang, and Claire Cardie. 2019. Multi-source cross-lingual model transfer: Learning what to share. In *Proceedings of the 57th Annual Meeting of the Association for Computational Linguistics*, pages 3098–3112, Florence, Italy. Association for Computational Linguistics.

Zixiang Chen, Yihe Deng, Huizhuo Yuan, Kaixuan Ji, and Quanquan Gu. 2024. Self-play fine-tuning converts weak language models to strong language models. *arXiv preprint arXiv:2401.01335*.

Alexis Conneau, Kartikay Khandelwal, Naman Goyal, Vishrav Chaudhary, Guillaume Wenzek, Francisco Guzmán, Edouard Grave, Myle Ott, Luke Zettlemoyer, and Veselin Stoyanov. 2020. Unsupervised cross-lingual representation learning at scale. In *Proceedings of the 58th Annual Meeting of the Association for Computational Linguistics*, pages 8440–8451, Online. Association for Computational Linguistics.

Bosheng Ding, Chengwei Qin, Ruochen Zhao, Tianze Luo, Xinze Li, Guizhen Chen, Wenhan Xia, Junjie Hu, Anh Tuan Luu, and Shafiq Joty. 2024. Data augmentation using LLMs: Data perspectives, learning paradigms and challenges. *arXiv preprint arXiv:2403.02990*.

Elvis Dohmatob, Yunzhen Feng, Pu Yang, Francois Charton, and Julia Kempe. 2024. A tale of tails: Model collapse as a change of scaling laws. *Preprint*, arXiv:2402.07043.

Chenhe Dong, Yinghui Li, Haifan Gong, Miaoxin Chen, Junxin Li, Ying Shen, and Min Yang. 2022. A survey of natural language generation. *ACM Comput. Surv.*, 55(8).

Abhimanyu Dubey, Abhinav Jauhri, Abhinav Pandey, Abhishek Kadian, Ahmad Al-Dahle, Aiesha Letman, Akhil Mathur, Alan Schelten, Amy Yang, Angela Fan, et al. 2024. The LLaMA 3 herd of models. *arXiv preprint arXiv:2407.21783*.

Julen Etxaniz, Oscar Sainz, Naiara Perez, Itziar Aldabe, German Rigau, Eneko Agirre, Aitor Ormazabal, Mikel Artetxe, and Aitor Soroa. 2024. Latxa: An open language model and evaluation suite for Basque. *Preprint*, arXiv:2403.20266.

Lucy Evans, William Lamb, Mark Sinclair, and Beatrice Alex. 2022. Developing automatic speech recognition for Scottish Gaelic. In *Proceedings of the 4th Celtic Language Technology Workshop within LREC2022*, pages 110–120, Marseille, France. European Language Resources Association.

Matúš Falis, Aryo Pradipta Gema, Hang Dong, Luke Daines, Siddharth Basetti, Michael Holder, Rose S Penfold, Alexandra Birch, and Beatrice Alex. 2024. Can GPT-3.5 generate and code discharge summaries? *Journal of the American Medical Informatics Association*, 31(10):2284–2293.

Emilio Ferrara. 2023. Should ChatGPT be biased? Challenges and risks of bias in large language models. *First Monday*.

Philip Gage. 1994. A new algorithm for data compression. *C Users J.*, 12(2):23–38.

Hila Gonen, Shauli Ravfogel, and Yoav Goldberg. 2022. Analyzing gender representation in multilingual models. In *Proceedings of the 7th Workshop on Representation Learning for NLP*, pages 67–77, Dublin, Ireland. Association for Computational Linguistics.

Xu Guo and Yiqiang Chen. 2024. Generative AI for synthetic data generation: Methods, challenges and the future. *Preprint*, arXiv:2403.04190.

Perttu Hämäläinen, Mikke Tavast, and Anton Kunnari. 2023. Evaluating large language models in generating synthetic HCI research data: A case study. In *Proceedings of the 2023 CHI Conference on Human Factors in Computing Systems*, CHI '23, New York, NY, USA. Association for Computing Machinery.

Kenneth Heafield, Ivan Pouzyrevsky, Jonathan H. Clark, and Philipp Koehn. 2013. Scalable modified Kneser-Ney language model estimation. In *Proceedings of the 51st Annual Meeting of the Association for Computational Linguistics (Volume 2: Short Papers)*, pages 690–696, Sofia, Bulgaria. Association for Computational Linguistics.

Kung Yin Hong, Lifeng Han, Riza Batista-Navarro, and Goran Nenadic. 2024. CantonMT: Cantonese to English NMT platform with fine-tuned models using synthetic back-translation data. *Preprint*, arXiv:2403.11346.

Raisa Islam and Owana Marzia Moushi. 2024. Gpt-4o: The cutting-edge advancement in multimodal LLM. *TechRxiv*.

Ran Iwamoto and Hiroshi Kanayama. 2024. LLM neologism: Emergence of mutated characters due to byte encoding. In *Proceedings of the 17th International Natural Language Generation Conference*, pages 24–29, Tokyo, Japan. Association for Computational Linguistics.

Ziwei Ji, Nayeon Lee, Rita Frieske, Tiezheng Yu, Dan Su, Yan Xu, Etsuko Ishii, Ye Jin Bang, Andrea Madotto, and Pascale Fung. 2023. Survey of hallucination in natural language generation. *ACM Comput. Surv.*, 55(12).

Pratik Joshi, Sebastin Santy, Amar Budhiraja, Kalika Bali, and Monojit Choudhury. 2020. The state and fate of linguistic diversity and inclusion in the NLP world. In *Proceedings of the 58th Annual Meeting of the Association for Computational Linguistics*, pages 6282–6293, Online. Association for Computational Linguistics.

Mahammed Kamruzzaman, Md. Minul Islam Shovon, and Gene Louis Kim. 2024. Investigating subtler biases in LLMs: Ageism, beauty, institutional, and nationality bias in generative models. *Preprint*, arXiv:2309.08902.

Viet Lai, Nghia Ngo, Amir Pouran Ben Veyseh, Hieu Man, Franck Dernoncourt, Trung Bui, and Thien Nguyen. 2023. ChatGPT beyond English: Towards a comprehensive evaluation of large language models in multilingual learning. In *Findings of the Association for Computational Linguistics: EMNLP 2023*, pages 13171–13189.

William Lamb. 2008. *Scottish Gaelic Speech and Writing: Register Variation in an Endangered Language*. Cló Ollscoil na Banríona, Belfast.

William Lamb. 2024. *Scottish Gaelic: A Comprehensive Grammar*. Routledge Comprehensive Grammars. Routledge, Oxon.

Kenneth Li, Tianle Liu, Naomi Bashkansky, David Bau, Fernanda Viégas, Hanspeter Pfister, and Martin Wattenberg. 2024. Measuring and controlling instruction (in)stability in language model dialogs. *Preprint*, arXiv:2402.10962.

Agustín Lucas, Alexis Baladón, Victoria Pardiñas, Marvin Agüero-Torales, Santiago Góngora, and Luis Chiruzzo. 2024. Grammar-based data augmentation for low-resource languages: The case of Guarani-Spanish neural machine translation. In *Proceedings of the 2024 Conference of the North American Chapter of the Association for Computational Linguistics: Human Language Technologies (Volume 1: Long Papers)*, pages 6385–6397.

Hugh MacEachen. 1967. Muncaidh a theich bhon pholitician, agus dithis sheann mhaighdeannan. School of Scottish Studies Archives: SA1967.6.A6. Available from `https://www.tobarandualchais.co.uk/track/109839?l`.

Alexandre Magueresse, Vincent Carles, and Evan Heetderks. 2020. Low-resource languages: A review of past work and future challenges. *arXiv preprint arXiv:2006.07264*.

Luca Massarelli, Fabio Petroni, Aleksandra Piktus, Myle Ott, Tim Rocktäschel, Vassilis Plachouras, Fabrizio Silvestri, and Sebastian Riedel. 2020. How decoding strategies affect the verifiability of generated text. In *Findings of the Association for Computational Linguistics: EMNLP 2020*, pages 223–235, Online. Association for Computational Linguistics.

Julie-Anne Meaney, Bea Alex, and William Lamb. 2024. Evaluating and adapting large language models to represent folktales in low-resource languages. In *The 4th International Conference on Natural Language Processing for Digital Humanities – NLP4DH 2024*.

Clara Meister and Ryan Cotterell. 2021. Language model evaluation beyond perplexity. In *Proceedings of the 59th Annual Meeting of the Association for Computational Linguistics and the 11th International Joint Conference on Natural Language Processing (Volume 1: Long Papers)*, pages 5328–5339, Online. Association for Computational Linguistics.

Marius Mosbach, Tiago Pimentel, Shauli Ravfogel, Dietrich Klakow, and Yanai Elazar. 2023. Few-shot fine-tuning vs. in-context learning: A fair comparison and evaluation. In *Findings of the Association for Computational Linguistics: ACL 2023*, pages 12284–12314, Toronto, Canada. Association for Computational Linguistics.

National Records of Scotland. 2022. Scotland's census 2022. `https://www.scotlandscensus.gov.uk`. Accessed: 2024-08-14.

Xuan-Phi Nguyen, Sharifah Mahani Aljunied, Shafiq Joty, and Lidong Bing. 2023. Democratizing LLMs for low-resource languages by leveraging their English dominant abilities with linguistically-diverse prompts. *arXiv preprint arXiv:2306.11372*.

OpenAI. 2024. GPT-4o system card. Accessed: 2024-10-04.

Sinead O'Connor and Helen Liu. 2024. Gender bias perpetuation and mitigation in AI technologies: Challenges and opportunities. *AI & SOCIETY*, 39(4):2045–2057.

Qianqian Qi, Lin Ni, Zhongsheng Wang, Libo Zhang, Jiamou Liu, and Michael Witbrock. 2024. Epic-level text generation with LLM through auto-prompted reinforcement learning. In *2024 International Joint Conference on Neural Networks (IJCNN)*, pages 1–8. IEEE.

Yiwei Qin, Graham Neubig, and Pengfei Liu. 2022. Searching for effective multilingual fine-tuning methods: A case study in summarization. *arXiv preprint arXiv:2212.05740*.

Haoran Que, Feiyu Duan, Liqun He, Yutao Mou, Wangchunshu Zhou, Jiaheng Liu, Wenge Rong, Zekun Moore Wang, Jian Yang, Ge Zhang, Junran Peng, Zhaoxiang Zhang, Songyang Zhang, and Kai Chen. 2024. Hellobench: Evaluating long text generation capabilities of large language models. *Preprint*, arXiv:2409.16191.

Alec Radford, Karthik Narasimhan, Tim Salimans, and Ilya Sutskever. 2018. Improving language understanding by generative pre-training.

Mohaimenul Azam Khan Raiaan, Md. Saddam Hossain Mukta, Kaniz Fatema, Nur Mohammad Fahad, Sadman Sakib, Most Marufatul Jannat Mim, Jubaer Ahmad, Mohammed Eunus Ali, and Sami Azam. 2024. A review on large language models: Architectures, applications, taxonomies, open issues and challenges. *IEEE Access*, 12:26839–26874.

Nathaniel Robinson, Perez Ogayo, David R. Mortensen, and Graham Neubig. 2023. ChatGPT MT: Competitive for high- (but not low-) resource languages. In *Proceedings of the Eighth Conference on Machine Translation*, pages 392–418, Singapore. Association for Computational Linguistics.

Teven Le Scao, Angela Fan, Christopher Akiki, Ellie Pavlick, Dusan Ilić-Sabo, et al. 2022. BLOOM: A 176b-parameter open-access multilingual language model. *arXiv preprint arXiv:2211.05100*.

Fabian David Schmidt, Ivan Vulić, and Goran Glavaš. 2022. Don't stop fine-tuning: On training regimes for few-shot cross-lingual transfer with multilingual language models. In *Proceedings of the 2022 Conference on Empirical Methods in Natural Language Processing*, pages 10725–10742.

Rico Sennrich, Barry Haddow, and Alexandra Birch. 2016. Neural machine translation of rare words with subword units. In *Proceedings of the 54th Annual Meeting of the Association for Computational Linguistics (Volume 1: Long Papers)*, pages 1715–1725.

Ilia Shumailov, Zakhar Shumaylov, Yiren Zhao, Nicolas Papernot, Ross Anderson, and Yarin Gal. 2024. AI models collapse when trained on recursively generated data. *Nature*, 631(8022):755–759.

Mark Sinclair, William Lamb, and Beatrice Alex. 2022. Handwriting recognition for Scottish Gaelic. In *Proceedings of the 4th Celtic Language Technology Workshop within LREC2022*, pages 60–70.

Rickard Stureborg, Dimitris Alikaniotis, and Yoshi Suhara. 2024. Large language models are inconsistent and biased evaluators. *arXiv preprint arXiv:2405.01724*.

Fahim Sufi. 2024. Generative pre-trained transformer (GPT) in research: A systematic review on data augmentation. *Information*, 15(2):99.

Yufei Tian, Tenghao Huang, Miri Liu, Derek Jiang, Alexander Spangher, Muhao Chen, Jonathan May, and Nanyun Peng. 2024. Are large language models capable of generating human-level narratives? *Preprint*, arXiv:2407.13248.

Robert D Van Valin and Randy J LaPolla. 1997. *Syntax: Structure, meaning, and function*. Cambridge University Press.

Ashish Vaswani, Noam Shazeer, Niki Parmar, Jakob Uszkoreit, Llion Jones, Aidan N Gomez, Łukasz Kaiser, and Illia Polosukhin. 2017. Attention is all you need. *Advances in neural information processing systems*, 30.

Jiaan Wang, Fandong Meng, Duo Zheng, Yunlong Liang, Zhixu Li, Jianfeng Qu, and Jie Zhou. 2022. A Survey on Cross-Lingual Summarization. *Transactions of the Association for Computational Linguistics*, 10:1304–1323.

Yequan Wang, Jiawen Deng, Aixin Sun, and Xuying Meng. 2023. Perplexity from PLM is unreliable for evaluating text quality. *Preprint*, arXiv:2210.05892.

Kaige Xie and Mark Riedl. 2024. Creating suspenseful stories: Iterative planning with large language models. *arXiv preprint arXiv:2402.17119*.

Canwen Xu, Daya Guo, Nan Duan, and Julian McAuley. 2023. Baize: An open-source chat model with parameter-efficient tuning on self-chat data. In *Proceedings of the 2023 Conference on Empirical Methods in Natural Language Processing*, pages 6268–6278, Singapore. Association for Computational Linguistics.

Kevin Yang, Yuandong Tian, Nanyun Peng, and Dan Klein. 2022. Re3: Generating longer stories with recursive reprompting and revision. *Preprint*, arXiv:2210.06774.

Hanqing Zhang, Haolin Song, Shaoyu Li, Ming Zhou, and Dawei Song. 2023. A survey of controllable text generation using transformer-based pre-trained language models. *ACM Computing Surveys*, 56(3):1–37.

Jinman Zhao, Yitian Ding, Chen Jia, Yining Wang, and Zifan Qian. 2024. Gender bias in large language models across multiple languages. *Preprint*, arXiv:2403.00277.

Wayne Xin Zhao, Kun Zhou, Junyi Li, Tianyi Tang, Xiaolei Wang, Yupeng Hou, Yingqian Min, Beichen Zhang, Junjie Zhang, Zican Dong, et al. 2023. A survey of large language models. *arXiv preprint arXiv:2303.18223*.

A Example of Synthetic and Genuine Narrative Text

System Message: You will receive a summary in English. Expand the summary into a longer traditional narrative in Scottish Gaelic.

User Message: The escaped monkey and the two old spinsters. A monkey escaped when the Politician sank and reached Gerinish. It went into the house of two old spinsters, who thought it was the captain. They gave it soup, which it spat out. It did the same with meat. It was a Friday, and one suggested it must be a Catholic, because they don't take meat on Fridays.

Synthetic Output from Fine-Tuned GPT-4o Model: *Nuair a chaidh am Politician fodha, theich muncaidh às. Chaidh e air tìr ann an Gearraidh na Mònadh. Bha dà chailleach thall an sin. Cha robh iad a' faicinn mòran dhaoine. Agus dh'fhalbh iad sìos gu taobh na tràghad a' coimhead dè bha a' tachairt agus chunnaic iad am muncaidh a' tighinn suas bhon tràigh. 'Ò,' thuirt tè dhiubh, 'seo fear de na mairbh a thàinig beò.' 'Ò, 's e,' thuirt an tè eile. 'Cò th' ann?' 'Tha mi cinnteach gur e am maighstir-sgioblaid a th' ann.' 'Ò, 's e,' thuirt i fhèin. 'Dè nì sinn ris?' 'Gabhamaid a-staigh e.'*

Thàinig am muncaidh suas chun an taighe agus dh'fhosgail iad an doras is ghabh iad a-staigh e. Chuir iad sìos aig an teine e. Thug iad brot dha agus shùisg e air feadh an ùrlair e. Thug iad feòil dha agus shùisg e air feadh an ùrlair i. Bha Dihaoine ann. Thuirt tè dhiubh: 'Tha mi cinnteach gur e Caitligeach a th' ann, agus nach eil e ag ithe feòla Dihaoine.'

Human Translation of Synthetic Output from Fine-Tuned GPT-4o Model: When the Politician sank, a monkey escaped. He went ashore in Garrynamonie. There were two old ladies over there. They did not see many people. And they went down to the beach to see what was happening and they saw this monkey coming up from the beach. 'Oh,' said one of them, 'this is one of the dead who survived.' 'Oh, yes,' said the other. 'Who is it?' 'I'm sure he's the captain.' 'Oh, it is,' she said herself. 'What shall we do with it?' 'Let's take him in.' The monkey came up to the house and they opened the door and took him inside. They put him down at the fire. They gave him soup and he spat it all over the floor. They gave him meat and he spat it all over the floor. It was Friday. One of them said: 'I'm sure he's a Catholic since he doesn't eat meat on Friday.'

Synthetic Output from Baseline GPT-4o Model: *Bha muncaidh air teicheadh nuair a chaidh am Poileataigs fodha agus ràinig e Geàrraidh na h-Aibhne. Chaidh e a-steach do thaigh dà sheann mhaighdean, a bha den bheachd gur e an caiptean a bh' ann. Thug iad brot dha, ach shèid e a-mach e. Rinn e an aon rud leis a' mhart-fheòil. Bha Dihaoine ann, agus mhol tè dhiubh gum feumadh e bhith na Chaitligeach, oir cha ghabh iad feòil air Dihaoine.*

A-nis, leig dhuinn an sgeulachd seo a leudachadh ann an Gàidhlig thraidiseanta.

Bha là fada is duilich aig muinntir Geàrraidh na h-Aibhne nuair a chaidh am bàta, ris an canar am Poileataigs, fodha ann an stoirm mhòr. Ach cha robh fios aig duine sam bith gun robh muncaidh air bòrd a' bhàta sin. Bha an t-ainmhidhean glic seo air teicheadh às an tubaist agus rinn e air tìr gu sàbhailte. An dèidh siubhal tro fhiadh-bheatha na sgìre, ràinig e mu dheireadh taigh beag air iomall a' bhaile far an robh dà sheann mhaighdean a' fuireach.

Nuair a chunnaic na seann mhaighdeanan am muncaidh a' tighinn a-steach don taigh aca, bha iad cinnteach gur e an caiptean bhon bhàta briste a bh' ann. "Thig a-steach, thig a-steach," thuirt tè dhiubh gu càirdeil, "feumaidh tu bhith sgìth is acrach." Dh'fhairich iad co-fhaireachdainn mòr ris agus chuir iad romhpa biadh blàth ullachadh dha.

Thug iad brot blasta dha, ach nuair a dh'fheuch am muncaidh ri ithe, shèid e a-mach e le tàmailt. Bha na seann mhaighdeanan fo iongnadh ach smaoinich iad gur dòcha nach robh e dèidheil air brot. Mar sin, chuir iad pìos mòr de mhart-fheòil air beulaibh an aoigh neo-àbhaisteach aca. Ach cha b' fhada gus an do rinn am muncaidh an aon rud ris a' mhart-fheòil—shèid e air falbh i gun mòran beachd.

Bha na seann mhaighdeanan fo chlisg agus thòisich iad air bruidhinn ri chèile mu dheidhinn nan tachartasan neònach seo. "Tha rudeigin gu math neònach mun duine seo," thuirt tè dhiubh. "Tha e Dihaoine an-diugh," thuirt am fear eile gu h-obann, "agus tha mi cinnteach gur e Caitligeach a th' ann. Chan eil Caitligich ag ithe feòil air Dihaoine."

Agus mar sin, dh'aontaich iad gum bu chòir dhaibh urram a thoirt do chreideamh am "caiptein" ùr aca agus thòisich iad air biadh freagarrach ullachadh dha airson Dihaoine—gun fheòil idir.

Mar sin thàinig deireadh air latha iongantach anns an robh dà sheann mhaighdean agus muncaidh teicheadh ag ionnsachadh mu dheidhinn cho cudromach sa tha urram agus tuigse eadar daoine (agus ainmhidhean) bho dhiofar chùl-raointean agus creideamhan.

Human Translation of Synthetic Output from Baseline GPT-4o Model: A monkey had escaped when the Politics sank and he arrived in Garynahine [NB: this is a township in Lewis, many islands away.]. He went into the house of two old maidens, who believed that he was the captain. They gave him soup, but he spat it out. He did the same thing with beef. It was Friday, and one of them suggested that he must be a Catholic, since they don't eat meat on Friday.

Now, allow us to expand this story in traditional Gaelic.

It was a long and difficult day for the people of Garynahine when the boat called Politics [*sic.*] sank in a big storm. But nobody knew that there was a monkey on board that vessel. This clever animals [*sic.*] had fled from the accident and he managed to get to land safely. After travelling through the wildlife [*sic.*] of the region, he finally arrived at a small house on the edge of the township where two old maidens were living.

When the old maidens saw the monkey coming into their house, they were sure that he was the captain of the ship. "Come in, come in," said one of them kindly, "you must be tired and hungry." They felt great sympathy for him and they set out to prepare some warm food for him.

They gave him some tasty soup, but when the monkey tried to eat it, he spat it out with shame. The two old maidens were confused but they figured that he wasn't keen on soup. Then they put a big piece of beef before their unusual guest. But it wasn't long until the monkey did the same thing with the beef—he spat it out without further consideration.

The two old maidens were startled and they began to discuss these strange events. "There is something very unusual about this fellow," one of them said. "It is Friday today," the other one [NB: masculine pronoun used] said suddenly, "and I'm sure that he is a Catholic. Catholics don't eat meat on Friday."

Then they agreed that they should respect the beliefs of their new "captain" and they began to prepare appropriate food for him for Friday–without any meat.

As such, the extraordinary day ended in which two old maidens and a monkey escaping [*sic.*] were learning about how important it is for respect and understanding to exist between people (and animals) from different backgrounds and belief-systems.

Human Transcription of Original Audio (MacEachen, 1967): *Uel bha siud ma-tà bho chionn trì bliadhna fichead air ais, cha chreid mi nach e a th' ann bhon a chaidh Am Politician air an sgeir ann an Caolas Èirisgeigh. Agus co-dhiù nuair a chaidh i air an sgeir, dh'fhàg an sgiobair is an criubha, dh'fhàg iad i uile gu lèir. Agus gu dè a bh' ac' air bòrd ach muncaidh. Agus theich am muncaidh 's rinneadh a thaighean cuideachd. Is bha e caran mu chuairt air feadh an eilein an sin – air ais 's air aghaidh – is cha robh e faighinn gu robh e dèanadh a dhachaigh an àite sam bith. Ach co-dhiù thàinig e dhan taigh a bha seo ann an Gèirinis. Agus bha dà sheann mhaighdeann ann, Ceit agus Mòr. Agus bha iad a' gabhail an dìnnear agus mar a tha fhios againn uile gu lèir bha coupons air a h-uile nì an àm a' chogaidh agus chan fhaigheadh tu ach beagan de dh'fheòil is beagan dhen a h-uile sìon. 'S ann le na coupons a bha thu ga fhaighinn, co-dhiù. Agus thàinig e ... bha iad a' gabhail an dìnnear, an dà sheann mhaighdeann a bha seo, agus dìreach cò thàinig a-staigh an dorast ach e seo, an giobal a bha seo, agus choimhead na boireannaich mu chuairt agus thuirt iad riutha fhèin, 'Ò an duine bochd. Sgiobair a' bhàta is chaidh i air an sgeir. Bheir sinn dha a dhìnnear.' Dh'èirich Mòr agus fhuair i soup dhan duine a thàinig a-staigh, dhan choigreach a thàinig a-staigh, agus bha ... shuidh e aig a' bhòrd còmhla riutha. Fhuair e spàin 's dar a thòisich e air blasad air an soup, chuireadh e dhan bheul e is bheireadh e a-mach e 's spriodadh e air feadh an taigh e. Agus an sin, thuirt an dàrna tè ris an tè eile, 'Cha thoil leis soup,' thuirt i. 'Bheir sinn dha feòil 's buntàta.' Thug iad feòil 's buntàta dha. Thòisich cagnadh. Thilgeadh e pìos dheth an-dràsta air Mòr is pìos eile air Ceit agus ... nuair a bheireadh e treis air a' chagnadh. 'Ò an creutair, tha mise tuigsinn dè a th' ann,' thuirt i, 'ceart gu leòr. 'S e Dihaoine a th' ann an diugh! 'S e Pàpanach a th' ann is cha ghabh e brod na feòil an diugh,' thuirt i.*

Machine-assisted Translation of Original Audio: Well, it must've been about twenty-three years ago, I reckon, when the Politician ran aground on the skerry at the Strait of Eriskay. Anyway, when it hit the skerry, the skipper and the crew just up and abandoned it. And what did they leave behind but a monkey. The monkey ran off and made itself at home on the island, wandering here and there, not really able to settle anywhere. Eventually, it made its way to a house in Gerinish, where two old spinsters, Kate and Sarah, were sitting down for their dinner. Now, as we all know, during the war everything was rationed – you could only get a little bit of meat or anything else, and you needed coupons for everything. Anyway, as they were eating, in comes this ragamuffin through the door. The women turned and said to themselves, 'Oh, the poor man. It must be the skipper from the boat that went aground on the skerry. Let's give him something to eat.' So, Sarah got up and fetched a bowl of soup for the stranger, who sat down at the table with them. He took a spoonful, but as soon as it touched his mouth, he spat it right out, spraying it all over the house. One of the women looked at the other and said, 'He doesn't like soup. Let's give him some meat and potatoes.' So, they gave him meat and potatoes. He started chewing but, after a bit, he spat it out too – first on Sarah, then on Kate. 'Oh, the poor creature,' she said. 'I understand now – it's Friday! He's Catholic and can't have any meat today.'

A Pragmatic Approach to Using Artificial Intelligence and Virtual Reality in Digital Game-Based Language Learning

Monica Ward[1], Liang Xu[1], Elaine Uí Dhonnchadha[2]
[1]Dublin City University, Ireland
[2]Trinity College Dublin, Ireland
{monica.ward, liang.xu}@dcu.ie
uidhonne@tcd.ie

Abstract

Computer Assisted Language Learning (CALL) applications have many benefits for language learning. However, they can be difficult to develop for low-resource languages such as Irish and the other Celtic languages. It can be difficult to assemble the multidisciplinary team needed to develop CALL resources and there are fewer language resources available for the language. This paper provides an overview of a pragmatic approach to using Artificial Intelligence (AI) and Virtual Reality (VR) in developing a digital game-based language learning (DGBLL) app for Irish. This pragmatic approach was used to develop Cipher - a DGBLL app for Irish (Xu et al, 2022b) where a number of existing resources including text repositories and NLP tools were used. In this paper the focus is on the incorporation of Artificial Intelligence (AI) technologies including AI image generation, text-to-speech (TTS) and Virtual Reality (VR), in a pedagogically informed manner to support language learning in a way that is both challenging and enjoyable. Cipher has been designed to be language independent and can be adapted for various cohorts of learners and for other languages. Cipher has been played and tested in a number of schools in Dublin and the feedback from teachers and students has been very positive. This paper outlines how AI and VR technologies have been utilised in Cipher and how it could be adapted to other Celtic languages and low-resource languages in general.

1 Introduction

Computer-Assisted Language Learning (CALL) can be beneficial for language learners (Beatty, 2013). It can enable them to learn a language, either independently or in conjunction with a teacher. CALL resources can be used anytime and anywhere and at any pace. Using CALL resources can increase motivation for learners, enable them to repeat activities as often as they like and there is an element of privacy, so learners feel less inhibited about making mistakes. Learners of all language can benefit from using CALL resources. However, not all language learners have access to good quality, engaging CALL resources. There is a wealth of resources available for the world's most commonly taught languages, particularly English, but this is not the case for Less Commonly Taught Languages (LCTLs) such as Irish (Ward, 2016) and other Celtic languages. There are many reasons for this, including the difficulty of gathering a multidisciplinary team for the development of CALL resources and the lack of language technologies available for LCTLs (Ward, 2015a).

This paper focuses on a pragmatic approach to the development of Cipher, a CALL resource for Irish that combines several Artificial Intelligence (AI) technologies and VR to produce an engaging digital game-based language learning app for the Irish language. With limited resources available, it is important to use AI technologies and VR in a targeted and pedagogically sound manner to enhance specific elements of the app.

The Cipher app focuses on building vocabulary and reading. It is a game in which players have to find words in a story that have been put under a magic spell by an evil character and they must identify which spell the evil character has used. Players get points as they progress through the game and hints are available if necessary. The player is presented with various challenges that require them to notice spelling and word order. Although the main aim is to assist in language learning, the fun aspect of playing a game is paramount at all times.

Proceedings of the 5th Celtic Language Technology Workshop (CLTW 5), pages 27–34
Abu Dhabi, UAE (Online), January 20, 2025

This paper provides an overview of the technologies used in the app, which include NLP tools to assess the quality and level of the texts used in the game, text-to-speech (TTS) tools to provide audio for the game, the AI-image generation tool to produce images for the game and the VR tool used to produce an initial 3D version of the game. While this paper focuses on the Irish language version of Cipher, the game engine is language independent, and the app could be customised for other languages.

2 Background

2.1 CALL for Irish

The development of CALL resources for any language is difficult. Ideally, the CALL development team will be a multidisciplinary one with language teachers, linguists, software developers, user interface designers, Natural Language Processing (NLP) specialists and learners all being members of the team. Ideally, there will be a wealth of digital resources for the language, including texts, audio resources and NLP tools for the language. However, in the case of LCTLs, which includes all the Celtic languages, these ideal conditions do not prevail. It can be very difficult to assemble a multidisciplinary team and there are fewer digital resources for the language. In this scenario, it is really important to work strategically and to leverage existing resources for the language and to repurpose existing resources for other languages in the development of CALL resources for the language (Ward, 2015b). Each language has a different profile of resources available for CALL development. In the case of Irish there were a number of important resources that we were able to draw on. There is a collection of digital texts in the Dúchas.ie Schools Collection archive. This is a collection of folklore materials that were written by primary school children aged 12-14 in the 1930's. There is abair.ie, a high quality text-to-speech (TTS) tool for Irish that can produce audio files in three dialects and at varying speeds, which is particularly useful for language learning. There is a comprehensive morphological analyser and generator, and rule-based part-of-speech tagger (Uí Dhonnchadha & Van Genabith, 2006) that provides the grammatical features of words in the stories that are necessary for some of the ciphers (spells). Compared with better resourced languages, these resources do not provide the same coverage, but they have been very useful for the development of CALL resources for the language. These language-specific resources are now being combined with general-purpose AI language technologies to produce a more rounded application as will be outlined in the rest of the paper.

2.2 AI Technologies and CALL

AI has been discussed in the CALL research community for many years (e.g. Schulze, 2008; Ward, 2017). Natural Language Processing (NLP) technologies can contribute greatly to the development of CALL resources. NLP tools can be used in error checkers (including spelling and grammar checkers). They can be used to provide dictionary information for words and phrases in a text. They can be used to check the complexity of a piece of text in terms of lexical and grammatical complexity and this can be used to determine the suitability of a text for a given learner level. Bryant et al., (2023) provide a comprehensive overview of the use of NLP technologies in error correction. Gillespie (2020) charts the use of NLP in CALL research. To date, the use of AI technologies in CALL was relatively limited, but as the technologies have improved and become more accessible for non-AI experts, they are being increasingly used in the development of CALL resources.

Text to Speech (TTS) tools convert digital text into audio format. This can be really helpful in the language learning process, particularly if the language being studied uses a different writing system or orthography than the learner's first language (L1). While Irish uses the Latin alphabet, the orthography of Irish is different from English and this can be challenging for learners who tend to transfer their understanding of English orthography to Irish phonology. A further difficulty is that until recently, Irish orthography has not been explicitly explained to learners (in many primary and secondary school settings), and this makes it hard for students to read a word and understand how it is pronounced. Being able to read and hear a word pronounced can be really helpful for students.

Images can help in the comprehension of a text (Schroeder et al., 2011), especially if they are closely aligned with the content of the text. However, it can be challenging to find suitable images and it is expensive and time consuming to design and draw images manually if suitable images cannot be found. One solution to this problem is to use AI generated images. Using AI generated images enables the CALL development team to create images that align with the text and create the desired atmosphere. For example, AI image generators can create images that are very realistic, cartoon-like or more ephemeral depending on what is required. The process of creating the desired image may not be entirely straightforward and care and thought are required to develop the prompts to the AI image generator in order to create the desired image.

2.3 Virtual Reality and CALL

Virtual Reality can help in the language learning process. Learners can be immersed in a virtual world where they can interact with the language. Being in a virtual world can help learners to forget their inhibitions about making mistakes and thereby overcome this barrier to learning a language. Another benefit of a VR learning environment is that the learner can 'be' in a world that does not exist in the real world. This could be a magical world or a world in the past or the future. These worlds can be exciting and engaging for learners, and CALL developers are starting to develop CALL resources using VR technologies.

2.4 Cipher: Faoi Gheasa - A Digital Game-Based Language Learning App for Irish

The main aims of this game are a) to increase user engagement and motivation for learning Irish, and b) to support the acquisition of Irish spelling, vocabulary and reading. We chose to use fiction, i.e., stories from folklore, mythology and traditional fairy tales, rather than non-fiction prose as it is more engaging for learners. The game is set in a magical world, where an evil character casts a spell on certain words in a text so that people will not be able to read and understand the text. These magic spells involve spelling the word backwards, swapping the first and last letter, doubling the last letter, or removing all vowels etc. The players have to find these enchanted words and identify which spell the evil character (Figure 5) has used on the words. This means that players have to pay close attention to words and to sound them in their heads. Initially we used a mix of real errors taken from primary school student writing, together with artificial errors such as spelling the words backwards (spells). In our early testing it became apparent that real spelling errors were too difficult for learners to spot, whereas finding the artificial errors, because they were pattern-based, was much more achievable and enjoyable. We decided to use ciphers (spells) only and this has a number of benefits, including the fact that learners are not exposed to real errors. Also, we can develop spells that draw attention to language specific issues such as accented vowels, initial mutations and noun gender.

As players identify the spells and enchanted words, they gain points and progress to the next page in a story. Before players can progress to the story element of the game they must complete word challenges to become familiar with key words in the story and with the spells. Figure 1 shows a screenshot of a word challenge in the vocabulary priming element of the game where *ocras* (hunger) is under the *Méadú Guta* (Vowel Sprout) spell, all of the vowels have become accented vowels, while Figure 2 shows a screenshot of the main story element of the game, with some possible spells beneath. There is an example of a page from the Hansel and Gretel story where the highlighted words are under a spell. The player has identified 5 of the 6 enchanted words, and has correctly identified the *Cúl Faoi Dhó* (Double Tail) spell and incorrectly chosen *Iompú* (Reverse) in place of the correct *Tóin Aníos* (Bottom Up) spell.

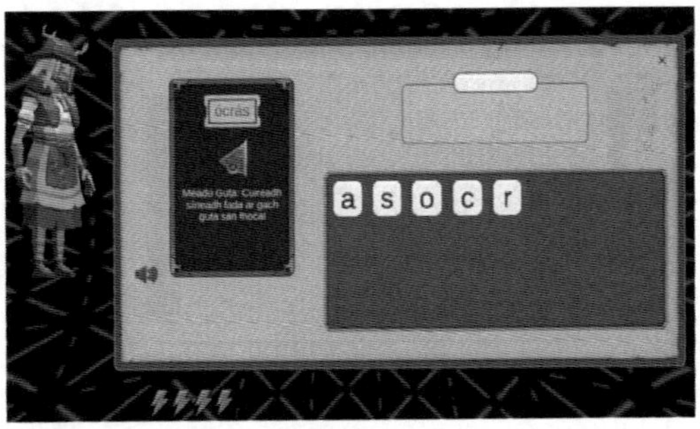

Figure 1: Cipher Vocabulary.

3 Methodology

The core Cipher team consisted of a game developer, an Irish NLP researcher and a CALL researcher. Several other researchers and developers contributed to specific aspects of the project. While each member of the team had relevant expertise, it was important to leverage the affordances of AI and VR tools and technologies to accelerate the game development process and enhance the game itself. A pragmatic approach was adopted whereby existing resources were reused or repurposed where possible and new tools were developed with limited, but targeted functionality.

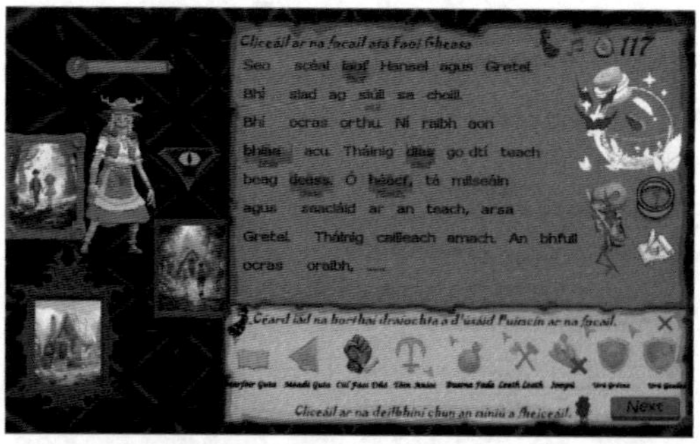

Figure 2: Cipher Reading.

3.1 Integration of AI Technologies in Cipher

Children learn a language in a physical and cultural context and with all of their senses. In this CALL application the aim is to involve as many of the senses as possible to support second language learning. Sight is involved through the use of imagery, hearing through the use of audio support for vocabulary learning and to explain the rules of the game, and touch and motion through the Virtual Reality interface. Unique cultural heritage is invoked through the use of folklore and mythology in the stories and in the physical VR environment.

3.2 Text Content Development

Existing and new resources were used in the development of Cipher for Irish. Existing texts which were digitized as part of the Dúchas Schools Collection were the basis of some of the Cipher stories. While these stories are captivating, they were written before the introduction of the current standard orthography and grammar for Irish and had to be converted to the current standard, An Caighdeán Oifigiúil (Rannóg an Aistriúcháin, 2017). Existing NLP tools were used to tag each word in a text with its correct part-of-speech (POS) tag. This was important for implementing some ciphers which target or avoid specific types of words. Another use of NLP tools was in checking the suitability of texts for the target audience. Cipher is targeted at beginners and false beginners[1], although it can be adapted for more advanced learners as well. It was essential that the texts were at the appropriate level of difficulty for players so they could understand the texts and progress comfortably through the game. Readability tools and datasets are readily available for English e.g. the Flesch Kincaid (Kincaid, 1975), Gunning Fog (Gunning, 1952) and many more[2]. However, new NLP tools had to be developed for the purpose of rating Irish texts for readability. This involved creating appropriate datasets, and devising a text ranking formula by calculating lexical and grammatical complexity features, (Uí Dhonnchadha et al., 2024) as well as using AI learning (Mc Cahill et al., 2024).

3.3 Image Support

Text-to-Image generation i.e., Midjourney[3] was used to create the AI generated images. AI image generators can generate almost any kind of image and a less realistic, more cartoon like image theme was chosen for the Cipher game. This was in keeping with the overall vibe of the game. The AI image generator was also used to create the images for each page of the stories as well the vocabulary element of the game. Approximately 50-70 images per story were created. Some images were easy to generate, e.g. trees or a river, whereas more abstract concepts, e.g. in hiding, famous etc., were more difficult to conceptualise and took numerous attempts to find prompts that generated suitable images. Photoshop was necessary as a final step to fix aspects of some images or to remove unwanted items from images, such as a car parked outside the witch's house.

3.4 Audio Support

The abair.ie text-to-speech (TTS) tool for Irish, was used to provide the audio files for the vocabulary element of Cipher. The game has an English, Irish and Chinese interface. In order to make the game more accessible for learners, in the English interface, audio instructions were provided to players. The English language audio files were generated using a specific character voice from ElevenLabs[4]. The intention is to provide audio instruction in Irish as part of the Irish interface.

[1] False beginners are learners who consider themselves to be beginners even though they already have some knowledge of the language.

[2] `https://www.linguisticanalysistools.org/`

[3] `https://discord.com/invite/midjourney`

[4] `https://elevenlabs.io`

This audio feature was added to reduce the cognitive load on players who may have difficulties reading the instructions as they can listen to them instead. The voice chosen for the instructions was witch-like, in keeping with the overall atmosphere of the game.

3.5 Integration of VR Technology in Cipher

The Cipher game is a 2D game that can be played on a tablet. However, a pilot 3D version of the vocabulary challenge element of the game has been developed to explore the use of VR technology in CALL for Irish. In the VR version of Cipher, the players still have to spell Irish words correctly to move through the game. Enchanted words from the Salmon of Knowledge story, appear in the magic book. The cipher is also given (see Fig. 3), which allows the player to mentally reconstruct the word, then they have to put the scrambled letters into the correct order on a table using their hands. This requires mental and physical activity. Meanwhile, the game is situated in the ancient mythical world of The Salmon of Knowledge. This variety of sensory input makes vocabulary learning more memorable. Unity[5] was used to develop the 3D version of Cipher and VR. Figure 3 shows a screenshot of the VR version of Cipher. It shows the word *tine* (fire) under the 'Vowel Sprout' (*Méadú Guta*) spell becoming 'tíné'.

Figure 3: Scrambled letters on a table and hand tracking in VR in an immersive folklore world.

3.6 Cipher Development Process

The initial version of Cipher was developed for English error correction and players had to select words that were spelt incorrectly in a text (Xu & Chamberlain, 2020). The Cipher team saw the potential of the game for language learning and decided to repurpose the game for Irish. This required finding and pre-processing Irish texts, the development of ciphers specific to Irish, and adding new game elements. The Irish version of Cipher taps into the 'spirit of the language' and is imbued with an ancient mythological Irish atmosphere. It has a vocabulary game at the start of each story, so that players can become familiar with key words in the text. There are AI-generated images and audio files to support the players. Hints are available to the players, but their points tally will decrease when they ask for help. If a player runs out of points, they can regain points by constructing a sentence using word bricks which will enable them to continue playing (Figure 4). A similar work brick approach was used successfully before with Irish (Purgina et al., 2017).

The Cipher development process is an iterative one. The core development team consisting of a game developer, an Irish NLP expert and a CALL developer, was supported by additional game developers, teachers and learners. When a new feature or improvement was added to the game, teachers and learners provided feedback which was used to inform the next development cycle of Cipher.

Figure 4: Sentence word bricks for Cipher.

Figure 5 An evil spirit

[5] https://unity.com

4 Results and Discussion

The Cipher game was positively received by students who preferred it over traditional classroom methods in a school-based survey (Xu et al., 2022a; Xu et al., 2024b). User feedback indicated a high level of satisfaction, with participants finding the game engaging and enjoyable, aligning well with their learning needs (Xu et al., 2022a). Cultural integration and responsive design elements within Cipher also contribute to its success as a language learning tool, with features like AI-generated visuals and VR increasing comprehension and immersion (Xu et al, 2023; Xu et al., 2024b). Cipher demonstrated learning gains in vocabulary acquisition, which was measured through the use of a double-baseline study involving approximately 60 primary students (Xu et al, 2024a).

There are several factors that contribute to the success of Cipher. These include adapting an existing resource (Cipher for English), the use of existing digital resources (e.g. Dúchas Schools Collection), the use of existing NLP resources (e.g. abair.ie, Irish morphological analyser), the development of new NLP tools (e.g. text readability tools for Irish) and the use of new AI technologies (e.g. AI-image generator, VR development toolkit).

Other factors include a modular approach and designing in a language-independent framework from the outset of the development process. This meant that changes could be made relatively easily and in an incremental manner. This iterative approach, which aligns with the agile approach to software development, is particularly suitable for contexts where there are a lot of unknown elements, which is true in the context of Cipher, where technology and the practicalities of a school setting must balance. The language-independent aspect means that it was easy to change the interface language, as well as the target language being studied. For example, an English interface is used for the instructions in the English-medium schools, with Irish being the interface language for the Irish-medium school.

Another important factor was the co-creation approach adopted by the Cipher team. This involved working with teachers and learners on a continuous basis throughout the development process. The teachers were able to help in selecting the words for the learning enhancement experiment and to give feedback on the Cipher game itself. The learners also seemed honest in their feedback, especially when there were parts they did not like. Their feedback was very helpful for the development team. The iterative and co-creation approach helped make Cipher an inclusive and resonant resource for Irish language acquisition.

It was relatively easy to use abair.ie and the elevenlabs.io TTS tool for the audio elements of Cipher. However, the other processes were less straightforward. The process of converting the Dúchas.ie texts to modern orthography (post 1958), and grammar conventions was semi-automated. While some of the conversions were straightforward (e.g., endings of verbs) and tools[6] are available to assist in the process, a manual post processing step was required to ensure the correctness of the conversion process. Currently there are approximately ten stories each with five to seven pages in the game.

The generation of the AI images while highly successful, was more time consuming than initially anticipated, as the prompts had to be carefully worded to ensure the creation of the desired images. AI image generators can generate images that reflect social biases and/or images that are inappropriate or weird. For example, asking the AI image generator to create images of witches led to images of very ugly women with warty notes or adult-themed images - neither type of image would have been suitable for primary school students. It was also challenging to ensure consistency of images across a story. Even something as straightforward as a boy and a girl, holding hands and walking in a wood was difficult (e.g. for Hansel and Gretel). Sometimes the images of the boy and the girl would not be consistent or the hands were not drawn correctly (hands are notoriously difficult for AI image generators). All images were pre-generated and vetted to ensure consistency and appropriateness, and in some cases Photoshop post-processing was necessary. Image creation has been carried out for two of the stories.

4.1 Limitations

There are several limitations that should be noted in the context of this paper. Firstly, the text,

[6] The following tools can convert between varieties of Irish: `https://github.com/kscanne/caighdean/blob/master/API.md` and `http://www.potafocal.com/cai/`

audio and image content is limited, and a much larger bank of stories needs to be developed. Secondly, while it was good to test Cipher in several different classrooms, the limited number of schools (three) means that current findings cannot be extrapolated to a wider cohort of students. Future testing will be required to validate these findings on a wider scale. The findings to date are promising and it will be interesting to see if these can be replicated with different cohorts of students.

The VR version of Cipher is currently at the pilot stage and the development of a VR game is more difficult than that of a 2D game due to the inherently more difficult programming process. However, in anticipation of further 3D developments, the 2D version of the game has been designed with VR in mind. The positive feedback to date on the VR version has given the Cipher development team encouragement for further developments to the 3D version of Cipher (Xu, 2024b).

5 Conclusions

In terms of adapting Cipher for other languages, there are several approaches that could be taken. In terms of the game itself, the Cipher system could be used to develop Cipher for another Celtic language. There may be an existing digital corpus of stores for the language or existing printed texts may be used as inspiration for suitable stories for Cipher. If the CALL developers have access to a POS-tagger , xml pos-tagged texts could be added to the Cipher system and this would speed up the development process. If xml pos-tagged files are not available, suitable texts could be manually tagged as a workaround. In terms of the audio files, if a TTS generator is available for the target language, that would be beneficial. If not, human recordings can be used instead. There are many TTS tools available for use in generating instructions in English, French and other well-resourced languages if this is an appropriate interface language for the game. AI-image generators are readily available, and although there are usage limits on the free versions, it is still possible to use them to generate appropriate images for stories. The VR tools are widely available and could be used by developers in other language contexts. In short, the more digital and AI resources available for the language, the easier it would be to create a Cipher game for the language. However, even if such resources do not exist, human-power can be used to generate a new version of Cipher for the language. Table 1 provides a summary of the resources reused, repurposed and developed as part of the development of Cipher, along with suggestions of how other languages could adopt a similar approach to the development of a Cipher version for the language.

Resource used	Existing/ Repurposed/ New	Comment
English language Cipher game	Repurposed	Could be repurposed for other languages
Dúchas collection	Existing and repurposed	Irish Folklore and culture focus
POS-tagger	Existing	An alternative would be a manually xml-tagged file
Readability tool	New	Semi-automatic
AI image generator	Existing	Language-independent, context aid
abair.ie	Existing	For Irish vocabulary pronunciation
English TTS tool	Existing	For in-game instructions
VR tool	Existing	Reinforce folklore and cultural immersion

Table 1: Overview of resources used in the development of Cipher

The integration of AI tools and technologies in the development of CALL resources for Irish can lead to the development of useful resources such as Cipher. Often CALL developers who work in the LCTL space can be intimidated by the challenge, but the approach adopted by the Cipher team demonstrates what is possible by using a combination of existing resources, development of new resources, along with a pragmatic and co-creation approach. Researchers working with other Celtic languages are encouraged to adopt a similar approach. The Cipher team would be happy to collaborate with other Celtic language researchers in developing a version of Cipher for their own language.

Acknowledgements

This research was supported by the Science Foundation Ireland Centre for Research Training in Digitally-Enhanced Reality (d-real) under Grant No. 18/CRT/6224. For the purpose of Open Access, the author has applied a CC BY public copyright licence to any Author Accepted Manuscript version arising from this submission. Thank you to the reviewers for their helpful suggestions

References

Beatty, K. (2013). Teaching & researching: Computer-assisted language learning. Routledge.

Bryant, C., Yuan, Z., Reza Qorib, M., Cao, H., Tou Ng, H. & Briscoe, T. (2023). Grammatical Error Correction: A Survey of the State of the Art. *Computational Linguistics* 2023; 49 (3): 643–701. https://doi.org/10.1162/coli_a_00478

Gunning, R. (1952). Technique of clear writing. McGraw-Hill.

Purgina, M., Mozgovoy, M., & Ward, M. (2017). MALL with WordBricks–building correct sentences brick by brick. CALL in a climate of change: adapting to turbulent global conditions–short papers from EUROCALL, 254-259.

Mc Cahill, L., Baltazar, T., Bruen, S., Xu, L., Ward, M., Uí Dhonnchadha, E., & Foster, J. (2024, May). Exploring Text Classification for Enhancing Digital Game-Based Language Learning for Irish. In Proceedings of the 3rd Annual Meeting of the SIGUL@ LREC-COLING 2024 (pp. 90-96).

Kincaid, J. P. (1975). Derivation of new readability formulas (automated readability index, fog count and flesch reading ease formula) for navy enlisted personnel. Chief of Naval Technical Training.

Schroeder, S., Richter, T., McElvany, N., Hachfeld, A., Baumert, J., Schnotz, W., Horz, H., & Ullrich, M. (2011). Teachers' beliefs, instructional behaviors, and students' engagement in learning from texts

Schulze, M. (2008). AI in CALL—Artificially inflated or almost imminent?. Calico Journal, 25(3), 510-527.

Uí Dhonnchadha, E., Bruen, S., Xu, L., & Ward, M. (2024, May). Empowering Adaptive Digital Game-Based Language Learning for Under-Resourced Languages Through Text Analysis. In Proceedings of the 10th Workshop on Games and Natural Language Processing@ LREC-COLING 2024 (pp. 6-13).

Uí Dhonnchadha, E. & Van Genabith, (2006) J. A Part-of-speech tagger for Irish using Finite-State Morphology and Constraint Grammar Disambiguation. LREC 2006.

Ward, M. (2015a). CALL and Less Commonly Taught Languages: Challenges and Opportunities. Research-publishing. net.

Ward, M. (2015b). Factors in sustainable CALL. WorldCALL: Sustainability and computer-assisted language learning, 132-151.

Ward, M. (2016). CALL and less commonly taught languages–still a way to go. CALL communities and culture: Short papers from EUROCALL, 468-473.

Ward, M. (2017). ICALL's relevance to CALL. CALL in a climate of change: adapting to turbulent global conditions–short papers from EUROCALL, 328.

Xu, L., and Chamberlain, J. (2020, May). Cipher: a prototype game-with-a-purpose for detecting errors in text. In Workshop on Games and Natural Language Processing (pp. 17-25).

Xu, L., Dhonnchadha, E. U., & Ward, M. (2022a). User experience study of" Cipher: Faoi Gheasa", a digital educational game for language learning and student engagement. In Proceedings of the 2nd Workshop on Games Systems (pp. 5-8).

Xu, L., Uí Dhonnchadha, E. & Ward, M. (2022b). Faoi Gheasa: an adaptive game for Irish language learning, *ACL 2022 ComputEL Workshop*, *Dublin, Ireland*, *26-27 May*, 2022

Xu, L., Andrade, M., Uí Dhonnchadha, E., and Ward, M. (2024a). Cipher in Classrooms: Evaluating Digital Game-Based Language Learning for Irish Vocabulary Acquisition. 13th International Games and Learning Alliance (GALA 2024) Conference. Serious Game Society, Berlin, Germany.

Xu, L., Du, H., Jia, S., Andrade, M., Ennis, C., Uí Dhonnchadha, E., and Ward, M. (2024b). Mythology Meets Technology: Transforming a 2D Game into a Virtual Reality Journey for Language Reconnection. IEEE 3rd International Conference on Intelligent Reality (ICIR 2024), Coimbra, Portugal.

Xu, L., Uí Dhonnchadha, E., and Ward, M. (2023). Harnessing the power of images in CALL: AI image generation for context specific visual aids in less commonly taught languages. In CALL for all Languages - EUROCALL 2023 Short Papers. Reykjavik, Iceland.

Fotheidil: an Automatic Transcription System for the Irish Language

Liam Lonergan[1], Ibon Saratxaga[2], John Sloan[1], Oscar Maharog [1], Mengjie Qian[3], Neasa Ní Chiaráin[1], Christer Gobl[1], Ailbhe Ní Chasaide [1]

[1]Phonetics and Speech Laboratory, Trinity College Dublin,
[2]HiTZ Basque Center for Language Technology, AhoLab,
University of the Basque Country UPV/EHU,
[3]Department of Engineering, University of Cambridge

[1]{llonerga, sloanjo,mahargbo, neasa.nichiarain, cegobl, anichsid}@tcd.ie, [2]ibon.saratxaga@ehu.eus, [3]mq227@cam.ac.uk

Abstract

This paper sets out the first web-based transcription system for the Irish language - Fotheidil, a system that utilises speech-related AI technologies as part of the ABAIR initiative. The system includes both off-the-shelf pre-trained voice activity detection and speaker diarisation models and models trained specifically for Irish automatic speech recognition and capitalisation and punctuation restoration. Semi-supervised learning is explored to improve the acoustic model of a modular TDNN-HMM ASR system, yielding substantial improvements for out-of-domain test sets and dialects that are underrepresented in the supervised training set. A novel approach to capitalisation and punctuation restoration involving sequence-to-sequence models is compared with the conventional approach using a classification model. Experimental results show here also substantial improvements in performance. The system will be made freely available for public use, and represents an important resource to researchers and others who transcribe Irish language materials. Human-corrected transcriptions will be collected and included in the training dataset as the system is used, which should lead to incremental improvements to the ASR model in a cyclical, community-driven fashion.

1 Introduction

Artificial intelligence (AI) has become a pervasive part of today's world. While AI undoubtedly brings many benefits, these benefits are felt primarily by speaker communities of the world's major languages. Speakers of minority languages have not been adequately serviced with technology that works for them and is appropriate for their needs.

Automatic speech recognition (ASR), the process of automatically transcribing speech into text, is a prime example of this disparity. While modern systems for English or Chinese approximate, or even improve upon, the performance of human transcription, for most languages Speech-to-Text does not exist. One of the largest barriers to developing ASR systems for minority languages is a lack of large, transcribed speech corpora. Recently, approaches leveraging large unlabelled speech corpora, such as semi-supervised learning (Zhang et al., 2020; Radford et al., 2023) and self-supervised learning (Baevski et al., 2020) have achieved state-of-the-art performance for common ASR benchmarks, and were beneficial for low-resource languages (DeHaven and Billa, 2022).

Speech-to-Text integrated technologies like automatic closed captioning on platforms such as YouTube and TikTok have been widely adopted by users of major languages. However, lesser-resourced languages are not included in such services. In light of this gap, we present Fotheidil[1] - a freely available web-based transcription system for the Irish language that utilises various speech-related AI components to transcribe long audio and video files. The structure of the paper is as follows: Section 2 outlines relevant background information; Section 3 details the system Interface; and section 4 describes the transcription pipeline, and the experiments carried out to improve Irish ASR performance using semi-supervised learning (SSL), as well as experiments carried out to train a Capitalisation and Punctuation Restoration (C&PR) model, which improves the legibility of the ASR outputs for the end-user; and finally, Section 5 contains the discussion and conclusions.

2 Background

2.1 Irish language

Irish, a Goidelic or Gaelic language, is a member of the Celtic branch of the Indo-European language family. Today, the Gaelic languages are spoken in small communities scattered mostly along the western seaboard of Ireland and the western islands

[1]https://fotheidil.abair.ie

Proceedings of the 5th Celtic Language Technology Workshop (CLTW 5), pages 35–45
Abu Dhabi, UAE (Online), January 20, 2025

of Scotland. The almost extinct Manx, which is currently being revived, is also a Goidelic language and is spoken on the Isle of Man.

The Irish language is highly inflected and has a complex phonological system. The language is diverse in its dialects and accents, with three regional dialects of Ulster (Ul), Connaught (Co) and Munster (Mu) and further sub-dialects, as well as the accents of non-native speakers i.e., learners and new speakers (Nn). The dialects vary significantly in terms of pronunciation, vocabulary and grammar and the phonology and syntactic structure of non-native speakers can often approximate that of English. Speaker variety is used here to describe the dialect or accent of a speaker.

2.2 ABAIR

The ABAIR initiative has been developing speech technology and applications to close the technology gap for the Irish language. Synthetic voices for the 3 major dialects of the languages of Ulster (Ul), Connacht (Co) and Munster (Mu) have been developed, with plans to expand this to further sub-dialects. Additionally, speech recognition systems for Irish have been developed with a sociolinguistic focus, by ensuring that we have adequate coverage of the different varieties of the language where possible and by evaluating our systems for their performance on speakers of different varieties.

2.3 Automatic Speech Recognition

ASR, the task of converting speech into text, has seen significant progress in recent years, due to advances in deep learning, access to hardware such as graphical processing units (GPU) and the increasing use of very large speech corpora. There are two conventional approaches to ASR - the traditional, modular approach, where the speech-to-text task is broken into the distinct components of acoustic modeling, pronunciation lexicon, and language modeling. The sub-modules are modeled independently and then combined in a decoding graph as a weighted finite-state transducer. In contrast, End-to-End (E2E) systems handle the entire speech-to-text task within a single model, directly learning the mapping from audio to text without the need for separate modules, offering a more streamlined but data-intensive approach. While E2E systems have surpassed modular systems in most performance benchmarks for ASR, the need to use large training corpora makes them less suitable for low-resource languages (Lonergan et al., 2024).

2.3.1 Semi-supervised learning

One of the most significant bottlenecks to the development of speech recognition for an under-resourced language is the availability of transcribed audio material to train an ASR system in a supervised manner. However, untranscribed speech is more readily available, due to the increasing proliferation of audio and video materials on the internet. Semi-supervised learning (SSL) is a paradigm that seeks to incorporate large unlabelled datasets in the learning framework to reduce the reliance on a large amount of labelled data. Among various SSL techniques applied to ASR, Noisy Student Teacher training (NST) has gained significant attention, achieving state-of-the-art performances across various datasets (Zhang et al., 2020; Park et al., 2020). Moreover, it has improved performance in code-switching ASR (Xi et al., 2024) and in low-resource ASR (Li and Vu, 2024).

Noisy Student Teacher training: in NST training, a teacher model is trained with the available labelled data. This model is used to generate pseudo-labels for the unlabelled dataset, which is combined with the labelled data to create a new training set for the student model. Noise is introduced to the new training set, forcing the student model to learn to reproduce the teacher model's outputs under noisy conditions, steering the model to learn more robust features that may better match the variability of real use.

2.4 Capitalisation and Punctuation Restoration

The output of the ASR system consists of raw text, using just lowercase characters, without punctuation symbols, acronyms or digits. This format is not very suitable in terms of readability and thus an additional processing is needed to restore proper capitalization and punctuation. Typically, capitalisation and punctuation restoration (C&PR) systems are word-level classifiers which implement either two separate classifiers for capitalisation and for punctuation, or a joint one. A review on these systems can be found in Păiş and Tufiş (2022).

In the case of Irish language, while punctuation rules are analogous to other western languages, capitalisation has its particularities, due to intial mutation, which is indicated orthographically by attaching different particles at the beginning of a word. These particles are one or two letters and are always written in lowercase, while the word keeps its original capitalisation: *i nGaeilge* (in Irish), *ón bhFrainc* (from France).

These specific cases are not covered by word level capitalisation models for other languages, which usually have just two classes indicating if the initial letter of the word should be lower or upper-cased. There are also character level capitalisation systems, but they perform worse and they are not so common.

Besides capitalisation and punctuation, the readability of the text is improved if numbers are written in digits instead of their textual form and acronyms are written in their condensed form instead of as they have been uttered by the speaker. Additionally, the use of specific symbols like percentage, currency, ordinal markers is also desirable. These fully formatted texts are often referred to as rich transcriptions.

3 Interface

User experience (UX) has been a key concern for the development of the Fotheidil interface. Users of the platform are likely to experience significant wait times while the files they uploaded undergo processing and recognition. These wait times have been shown to exhibit a negative logarithmic relationship with user satisfaction (Egger et al., 2012; Reichl et al., 2010). Mitigating the negative effects of long loading times in UX is typically tackled in two ways: speeding up processing; and reducing the user's frustration or perception of wait times. Increasing the processing speed is largely dependent on available hardware but can be aided by efficient infrastructure design. Reducing users' perception of waiting times can be achieved on the front end through effective use of loading visualisations (Kim et al., 2017). A description of both is provided below, with reference to Figure 1.

3.1 Backend

Three main back-end functionalities are hosted on separate Virtual Machines (VMs) to avoid competition for CPU resources. Media processing is carried out on one VM, voice activity detection, speaker diarisation and ASR on another, with database storage on a third. When a user uploads a media file, it is first directed to the Media Server where the audio is stripped/converted to a wav file with a 16000 Hz sampling rate and video compression takes place if necessary. The converted wav file is then sent to the Recognition VM

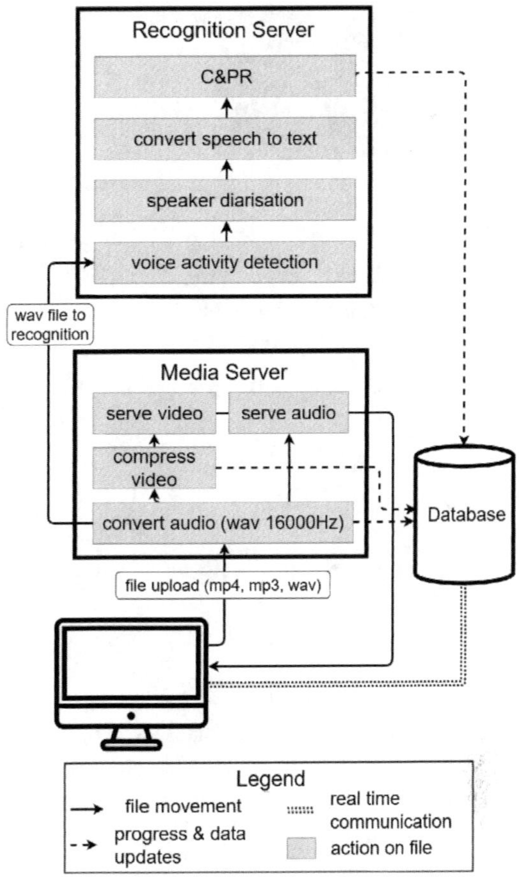

Figure 1: Infrastructure Diagram

where speaker diarisation and recognition models are hosted. Updates on the progress for each of the processes with potentially long wait times are continuously stored on the database.

Real Time Communication (RTC) between the front end and the database enables the user to view progress for each of these back-end processing steps. The main dashboard for interacting with, and editting, the processed data is shown in Figure 2. Users are able to edit the text, times and and speaker as well as download the output in pdf, docx or srt format.

4 Transcription Pipeline and Experiments

The transcription pipeline is a multi-step process, which brings together different systems to transcribe long audio files into text. The choice of the models used in some of these steps is made by weighing up their performance and efficiency.

The process is as follows:

i. Upload audio or video file.

ii. Extract or convert audio to 16kHz mono wav.

Figure 2: Main User Interface

iii. Voice activity detection to create segments.

iv. Speaker diarisation to assign speaker labels within speech segments.

v. Continuous segments of same speaker are joined.

vi. Segments are decoded with ASR system.

vii. ASR output is enhanced using a C&PR model.

While there are better performing alternatives that make use of GPUs, our web-based service is limited to CPU usage only. The voice activity detection and speaker diarisation systems are off-the-shelf, pretrained models and are detailed briefly in Sections 4.1 and 4.2, while the ASR and Punctuation and Capitalisaion models, which have been trained specifically for Irish, and these experiments are described in Sections 4.3 and 4.4.

4.1 Voice Activity Detection

Voice activity detection is the process of finding speech segments within an audio file. The voice activity detection (VAD) module used is Silero-VAD (Silero, 2024) - a robust, lightweight, pre-trained model. While PyAnnote is the conventional off-the-shelf choice for both VAD and speaker diarisation, it requires a GPU to be used efficiently. Silero-VAD offers a CPU only alternative with competitive VAD performance.

4.2 Speaker Diarisation

The goal of speaker diarisation is to assign a speaker label to each speech segment. A pretrained Kaldi-based speaker diarisation x-vector (Snyder et al., 2018) model[2] that is trained using augmented VoxCeleb1 and VoxCeleb2 datasets is used as part of this pipeline. The model has a reported EER performance of 3.7% on the Speakers in the Wild speaker identification test set.

4.3 Automatic Speech Recognition

Modular ASR approaches are often more suited to low-resource domains, as they do not require the same amount of data as E2E approaches. Additionally, modular systems are optimised to run efficiently on the CPU. Therefore, Kaldi-based DNN-HMM ASR models are used in our system and in the following experiments.

A baseline supervised model M_0 is trained using the supervised training set of 398h as described in Section 4.3.1 and detailed in Table 6 in the Appendix. To explore the usefulness of SSL for Irish ASR, a version of the approach outlined in Manohar et al. (2018), modified to include the noising element of NST, is tested in these experiments. The teacher model M_0 is used to decode the unlabelled set of 3230h in an undeterminised fashion, preserving the full decoding lattices. These lattices are rescored using a large n-gram language model (LM) and the best path through the rescored lattices is found. The best paths are taken as pseudo-labels and are combined with the supervised training set to create a semi-supervised training set. The student model M_1 is trained with the semi-supervised training set using the noising technique Spectral Augment (Park et al., 2015).

4.3.1 Data

The supervised acoustic training set comprises various datasets, as described in Table 6 in the Appendix with a breakdown of duration by speaker variety. Recordings used for ABAIR synthetic voices of the three dialects are used, totaling 41.4h (Syn). MíleGlór (MG) is an initiative for recording Irish speakers in the field and online using dialect-specific prompts, and a portion of 17.3h of this set is used. Additionally, two spontaneous speech (SS) corpora are combined, the large Corpas na Cainte Beo and the smaller Comhrá, totaling 259.7h. Audiobooks consisting of both professional and home recordings make up 36.6h. Caint Chonamara[3] (CCh), is a collection of conversations that was recorded in the Conamara area in 1964, representing rich dialectal speech of the Co dialect. Báiliúchán Béaloidis Árann (BBhÁ) is a folklore

[2]https://kaldi-asr.org/models/m8

[3]https://www.sksk.de/index.php/de/veroeffentlichungen-2/materialien/33-caint-chonamara

collection of conversational speech from the Aran Islands[4]. Datasets SS, AB, CCh and BBhÁ were aligned using the alignment protocol set out in Lonergan et al. (2024).

The unsupervised acoustic data consists of broadcast recordings from four Irish language radio shows featured on Raidió na Gaeltachta: Barrscéalta, which mainly features speakers of Ul Irish; Adhmhaidin, which primarily contains speakers of the Co dialect; An Saol Ó Dheas which largely features Mu speakers; and Nuacht a hAon, which has a mix of dialects. These recordings are downloadable in MP3 format from Raidió na Gaeltachta's podcast page. Silero-VAD, as described in Section 4.1, is used to find speech chunks for decoding and resulted in 3230h. A breakdown in duration by radio show is provided in Table 8 in the Appendix.

Five test sets are used to evaluate the system and details for these sets are given in Table 9 in the Appendix. The first two are portions of MG and SS taken from the training set corpora, ensuring no data leakage, and can be considered as in-domain tests. These sets are 10.2h and 28.2h in length respectively and their speaker variety breakdown in duration is detailed in Table 7 in the Appendix. Two additional out-of-domain test sets are the Irish test portions of CommonVoice (CV) (Ardila et al., 2020) and Fleurs-R (FL) (Ma et al., 2024) datasets. The quality of these datasets is markedly poor. Both datasets feature predominately non-native (Nn) speakers, and the texts for FL seem to be machine-translated English texts, which contain many foreign proper nouns. However, as they are publicly available and out-of-domain, we have included them here. They are 0.6h and 2.2h long respectively. Finally, 10 minutes each from the four radio shows (0.7h) from which the unsupervised dataset is created, were hand-labelled by the authors and are used here for evaluation (HL). While these do not appear in the unsupervised set, there is overlap in terms of speakers and likely content.

The text corpus of 36.6 million words used for LM training is comprised of normalised versions of the New Corpus of Ireland (Kilgarriff et al., 2006) (c. 30m words), the Bible (c. 0.1m words), Irish language Wikipedia texts (2.9m) and the supervised training set texts (4.6m).

[4]https://bba.duchas.ie/en/about/bba

4.3.2 Experiment

The acoustic model (AM) in the baseline ASR system M_0 is a Time-Delay Neural Network (TDNN) (Peddinti et al., 2025), trained using the 398h supervised train set (see Table 6) for 4 epochs. The initial alignment is produced by a triphone GMM-HMM trained with standard MFCC features, applying linear discriminative analysis (LDA), maximum likelihood linear transformation (MLLT), feature space maximum likelihood linear regression (fMLLR) and speaker adaptive training (SAT). The features for training the TDNN model are 40-dimensional high-resolution MFCCs stacked with 100-dimensional online extracted i-vectors. Two widely used on-the-fly data augmentation techniques for ASR – speed perturbation (Ko et al., 2015) with factors of 0.9, 1 and 1.1, and spectral augmentation (Park et al., 2015) were applied to augment the AM training data. The TDNN model consists of 6 TDNN layers with a hidden dimension size of 768. A pronunciation dictionary based on the Global rules, as described in Qian et al. (2022) and Lonergan et al. (2023a), which capture cross-dialect variation in the pronunciation of phonemes and morphemes, is used, along with a 4-gram LM, trained using the text corpus described in the last paragraph of Section 4.3.1.

As described in Section 4.3, pseudo-alignments for the unsupervised data are acquired by decoding the data using M_0, rescoring the undeterminised decoding lattices and finding the best path for each utterance. Rescoring is done using a 5-gram LM trained with the same texts described in Section 4.3.1. The resulting unsupervised and supervised alignments are combined with equal weighting. These semi-supervised alignments are then used to train M_1 with SpecAug for 6 epochs, with the same AM structure, lexicon and LM as M_0.

Recurrent neural network LMs (RNNLM) are beneficial in rescoring n-best lists generated by an ASR system (Xu et al., 2018). An RNNLM is trained on the text corpora listed in Section 4.3.1 and is used in these experiments. Where results including RNNLM are reported, they are labelled as (+LM).

4.3.3 Results

The WERs for in-domain test sets MG and SS have a relative improvement of 9% and 2% respectively with M_1. For the out-of-domain test sets CV and FL, the performance improves by 14% and 7% relatively. For HL, which more closely matches the

	MG	SS	CV	FL	HL
M_0	14.1	27.3	27.5	51.9	22.1
M_1	12.8	26.7	23.7	48.5	16.1
+LM	10.9	24.0	19.6	44.5	14.1

Table 1: ASR performance breakdown of models M_0 and M_1 of test sets and RNNLM rescoring (+LM).

	Overall	Ul	Co	Mu	Nn
M_0	14.1	18.5	14.0	10.8	13.2
M_1	12.8	15.3	13.1	10.2	12.6
+LM	10.9	12.7	11.6	8.8	10.4

Table 2: ASR performance breakdown by speaker variety of MíleGlór test set.

unsupervised data, there is a more dramatic relative performance improvement of 27%. RNNLM rescoring improves performance across the board and is complementary with the improved, semi-supervised acoustic model. Table 2 provides a breakdown of the performance on the MG set by speaker variety. The starkest improvement brought by the SSL approach to MG is the relative WER reduction of 17% for Ul speakers.

From these results, it is clear that SSL most significantly impacts performance on out-of-domain datasets, or domains more similar to the unsupervised training set (i.e. HL). Another noteworthy result is the boost in performance of Ul speakers, which is the least represented of the three dialects in the supervised training set (see Table 6). Previous studies on Irish dialect bias in ASR have shown that the Mu and Co dialects reinforce each other in terms of performance, whereas Ul, being a more distant dialect, is an outlier (Lonergan et al., 2023b). The improvement can be explained by Ul being well represented in the unsupervised set, indicating that such dialect bias can be alleviated using SSL. The improvements could be increased further by repeating this experiment multiple times, using the student of a previous experiment as the teacher for the next, or by increasing the size of the unlabelled dataset.

4.4 Capitalisation and Punctuation Restoration

In this work, we propose a novel approach to tackle the punctuation and capitalisation task, namely, a sequence-to-sequence (S2S) approach which will target all the rich transcription features in an unified way. The input for such a model is uncapitalised and unpunctuated i.e., as close as possible to the actual output of the ASR system. The output is the same text in its rich transcription format with correct capitalisation and punctuation, while also including digits and acronyms. The conventional approach is to use a classifier, which for each word in the input text, predicts whether the word should be followed by punctuation or should be capitalised, however as the input and output texts do not have a one-to-one word correspondence, a S2S architecture is more appropriate.

To that aim, our proposed model is a transformer based machine translation model, implementing the original model by Vaswani et al. (2017), which is based on attention mechanisms. We used the MarianNMT implementation (Junczys-Dowmunt et al., 2018) of this architecture.

For comparison purposes we have also tested a baseline system using a classification model (CLAS), Nvidia's Nemo Punctuation and Capitalisation Model[5]. This model features two token-level classifiers on top of a pre-trained BERT LM. For each word in the input text, the model predicts a punctuation mark that should follow the word, if any, and predicts also if the word should be capitalized or not. The output text is then regenerated applying the classification results to each input word. The classes of the original capitalisation model are expanded to include two additional classes for 2nd and 3rd letter capitalisation. The punctuation classifier has been trained with seven classes: commas, periods, question marks, exclamation marks, semicolons, colons and none.

4.4.1 Data

A text corpus of 5 million Irish sentences has been used to train the model. This corpus consists of the Irish section of the Paracrawl corpus (PC_ga) (Esplà et al., 2019), and the already mentioned New Corpus of Ireland (NCE), the Bible (BI) and the spontaneous speech corpus texts from the supervised training set, excluding the sentences used for testing (SS). The details are shown in table 11.

Four additional datasets have been used for evaluation: The Irish Language part of the FLoRes evaluation dataset (FO) (Team et al., 2022), commonly used for machine translation evaluation for low resourced languages and the MiléGlór (MG), Fleurs-R (FL) and CommonVoice (CV) evaluation datasets, employed also for the evaluation of

[5]https://docs.nvidia.com/nemo-framework/user-guide/latest/nemotoolkit/nlp/punctuation_and_capitalization.html

the ASR. The details of these databases are summarised in Table 10 in the Appendix.

The original text corpora were cleaned to create the training and evaluation datasets, removing non-standard characters, brackets, curly brackets and parenthesis, and standardising the use of spaces, quotes and so on. This clean text is the ground truth that will be used as target dataset in the case of our machine translation model. It will be referred as rich transcription (RT) dataset.

In order to obtain an input text as similar as possible to plain text output of an ASR system, the ground truth target was processed by the normalisation module of the Abair (Murphy et al., 2023) speech synthesis system. The normaliser converts every digit, acronym and some symbols into pronounceable texts, keeping the punctuation and capitalisation of the text. We will refer to this dataset as normalised rich transcript (NR). This dataset is used as ground truth to train the classifier system. The normalised text is then stripped out from any non-alphabetic character and lower cased, obtaining the input dataset (IN) for both of the systems.

4.4.2 Experiment Set-up

The proposed S2S model has a transformer architecture, with 8 heads, 6 encoding and 6 decoding layers, transformer dropout of 0.1 and tied embeddings. The training was done using label smoothing of 0.1, learning rate of $3 \cdot 10^{-4}$, warm-up stage and early stopping using cross-entropy, perplexity, BLEU detok, and CE-mean-words as validation metrics and a beam size of 6.

The baseline classifier system used the standard architecture of the NeMo model. It was trained using Google's pretrained BERT-base-uncased[6].

As the approach is a sequence to sequence task, to evaluate the systems, our main metric is a modified word error rate that uses the rich transcript as ground truth (instead the usual uncapitalised, unpunctuated text). We will denote it as WER_{pc} to distinguish it from the usual WER in ASR. We are also using character error rate (CER) to mean calculated with the rich transcript as target. Along with these metrics, we also use the BLEU score (Post, 2018), a common machine-translation metric which measures the similarity between generated and reference translations using n-grams.

[6]https://huggingface.co/google-bert/bert-base-uncased

	S2S			CLAS		
	Capt	Punct	WER_{pc}	Capt	Punct	WER_{pc}
FO	0.98	0.96	7.87	0.97	0.96	7.93
MG	0.98	0.95	8.36	0.97	0.95	9.69
CV	0.97	0.89	15.17	0.96	0.89	16.68
FL	0.97	0.96	8.27	0.97	0.96	8.53
ALL	0.98	0.95	8.40	0.97	0.95	9.38

Table 3: Capitalisation and punctuation accuracy and WER_{pc} using normalised rich transcripts (NR) as target.

4.4.3 Experiments and Results

We have performed two experiments to evaluate the proposed model using two metrics. Firstly, we compare the S2S approach with the baseline classifier approach. Due to the more limited capabilities of the classifier, and to allow a fair comparison of the performance of both models, we have used the normalised rich transcripts (NR) datasets as targets and the lower-cased, punctuation removed versions as input (IN). In this setup the input and output text are exactly the same with the only difference of punctuation marks and capitalisation.

The main metric used for comparison here is accuracy. This gives a general idea of the performance of the systems although the classes are severely unbalanced. The results in Table 3 show the accuracy and resulting WER_{pc} of both classifiers: capitalisation and punctuation. Both systems perform well with the proposed S2S system showing slightly higher accuracy and better WER_{pc}.

The second experiment setup reflects the actual use case of the restoration system: plain text at the input (the IN dataset) and full rich transcription (RT) at the output. Table 4 presents 3 groups of results: No C&P correspond to the comparison between the input (IN) and target outputs (RT) without any C&PR system and gives an idea of the disparity of both datasets, defining the maximum error level (or minimum BLEU) that will be corrected by the restoration systems. S2S and CLAS groups correspond to the results of both systems.

The results show that both systems are effective in C&PR, obtaining important reductions in the WER_{pc} and CER metrics. Our proposed S2S system reduces the WER_{pc} and CER by more than 50% and improves the BLEU more than 20 points for all datasets. S2S clearly outperforms the baseline classifier in this experiment, because it not only restores the casing and punctuation more effectively, but also changes digits or acronyms to a textual output that is closer to the target rich tran-

	No C&PR			S2S			CLAS		
	WER_{pc}	CER	BLEU	WER_{pc}	CER	BLEU	WER_{pc}	CER	BLEU
FO	22.2	7.7	64.7	7.9	1.9	85.1	13.62	5.31	80.1
MG	18.5	5.0	66.1	8.34	1.69	88.4	10.18	2.25	84.7
CV	25.6	5.7	61.4	18.29	4.94	82.9	16.78	3.19	79.9
FL	21.7	7.2	64.1	8.52	1.99	84.3	13.33	4.83	80.3
ALL	19.7	5.8	65.5	8.50	1.83	87.4	11.29	3.14	83.6

Table 4: C&PR performance with rich transcription (RT) as target.

	ASR	No C&PR			S2S		
	WER	WER_{pc}	CER	BLEU	WER_{pc}	CER	BLEU
MG	10.9	26.11	9.65	55.2	18.78	6.76	72.3
CV	19.6	40.43	16.59	45.5	34.75	15.63	63.0
FL	44.5	54.58	30.35	24.9	50.70	28.65	31.9

Table 5: Performance of the S2S C&PR system on ASR generated text with rich transcriptions (RT) as target.

scription. The error rates for S2S are below 9% for all the databases, except CV. This database contains a large number of very short, fragmentary sentences with inconsistent casing and punctuation, which may be interpreted as titles.

Finally Table 5 shows the effect of applying the S2S system to the actual output of the ASR. The input text is the plain text generated by the M_1(+LM) ASR model. The WER of these texts compared to the uncapitalised and unpunctuated references as shown previously in Table 1 is shown in the column ASR for readability. The results in column No C&PR show the WER_{pc} of the same texts when they are compared to the rich transcription. The columns under S2S show the results when the restoration system is applied. The final WERs are always lower than the accumulated WERs of the ASR and the S2S, suggesting that the degradation in the input text generated by the ASR does not impact in the performance of the S2S system.

5 Conclusion and Future Work

This paper constitutes an important step towards democratising speech-related AI technologies for the Irish language and its speakers. The ASR experiments have demonstrated that SSL learning is an attractive solution to improve performance for out-of-domain datasets and underrepresented dialects in the supervised training set. As stated, this improvement can be increased by iteratively repeating this process or increasing the size of the unlabelled dataset. Future work will explore SSL further.

The S2S model offers an elegant solution to the C&PR problem, improving significantly over the baseline due to its ability to effectively deal with the lack of a one-to-one relationship between the outputs of an ASR system and the rich transcriptions. The S2S model could additionally be trained using the output texts of the ASR systems so that it will be able to correct of some of the ASR errors. Furthermore, it can be trained to convert specific keywords, such as punctuation symbol names, currency or units, which would be very useful for dictation applications.

Acknowledgments

This work is part of the ABAIR initiative, which is supported by the Department of Tourism, Culture, Arts, the Gaeltacht, Sport and Media, with funding from the National Lottery, as part of the 20-year Strategy for Irish. The publication was partly funded by the Irish Research Council under grant number 214047. Part of this work was supported by the José Castillejo Mobility Programme of the Spanish Ministry of Science, Innovation, and Universities (CAS23/00294). The C&PR module is partially based on findings from the HiTZketan project of the UPV/EHU (COLAB22/13). We would like to especially acknowledge Dr. Gorka Labaka for his collaboration in the initial implementation of this system.

References

Rosana Ardila, Megan Branson, Kelly Davis, Michael Kohler, Josh Meyer, Michael Henretty, Reuben Morais, Lindsay Saunders, Francis Tyers, and Gregor Weber. 2020. Common voice: A massively-multilingual speech corpus. In *Proceedings of the*

Twelfth Language Resources and Evaluation Conference, pages 4218–4222, Marseille, France. European Language Resources Association.

Alexei Baevski, Yuhao Zhou, Abdelrahman Mohamed, and Michael Auli. 2020. wav2vec 2.0: A framework for self-supervised learning of speech representations. *Advances in Neural Information Processing Systems*, 33:12449–12460.

Mitchell DeHaven and Jayadev Billa. 2022. Improving low-resource speech recognition with pretrained speech models: Continued pretraining vs. semi-supervised training. *arXiv preprint arXiv:2207.00659*.

Sebastian Egger, Tobias Hossfeld, Raimund Schatz, and Markus Fiedler. 2012. Waiting times in quality of experience for web based services. In *2012 Fourth International Workshop on Quality of Multimedia Experience*, pages 86–96. IEEE.

Miquel Esplà, Mikel Forcada, Gema Ramírez-Sánchez, and Hieu Hoang. 2019. ParaCrawl: Web-scale parallel corpora for the languages of the EU. In *Proceedings of Machine Translation Summit XVII: Translator, Project and User Tracks*, pages 118–119, Dublin, Ireland. European Association for Machine Translation.

Marcin Junczys-Dowmunt, Roman Grundkiewicz, Tomasz Dwojak, Hieu Hoang, Kenneth Heafield, Tom Neckermann, Frank Seide, Ulrich Germann, Alham Fikri Aji, Nikolay Bogoychev, André F. T. Martins, and Alexandra Birch. 2018. Marian: Fast neural machine translation in C++. In *Proceedings of ACL 2018, System Demonstrations*, pages 116–121, Melbourne, Australia. Association for Computational Linguistics.

Adam Kilgarriff, Michael Rundell, and Elaine Uí Dhonnchadha. 2006. Efficient corpus development for lexicography: building the new corpus for ireland. *Language Resources and Evaluation*, 40:127–152.

Woojoo Kim, Shuping Xiong, and Zhuoqian Liang. 2017. Effect of loading symbol of online video on perception of waiting time. *International Journal of Human–Computer Interaction*, 33(12):1001–1009.

Tom Ko, Vijayaditya Peddinti, Daniel Povey, and Sanjeev Khudanpur. 2015. Audio augmentation for speech recognition. In *Proc. Interspeech 2015*, pages 3586–3589.

Chia-Yu Li and Ngoc Thang Vu. 2024. Improving noisy student training for low-resource languages in end-to-end ASR using CycleGAN and inter-domain losses. In *Proceedings of the 3rd Annual Meeting of the Special Interest Group on Under-resourced Languages @ LREC-COLING 2024*, pages 133–142.

Liam Lonergan, Mengjie Qian, Neasa Ní Chiaráin, Christer Gobl, and Ailbhe Ní Chasaide. 2023a. Cross-dialect lexicon optimisation for an endangered language ASR system: the case of Irish. In *Proc. Interspeech 2023*, pages 4865–4869.

Liam Lonergan, Mengjie Qian, Neasa Ní Chiaráin, Christer Gobl, and Ailbhe Ní Chasaide. 2024. Low-resource speech recognition and dialect identification of Irish in a multi-task framework. In *The Speaker and Language Recognition Workshop (Odyssey 2024)*, pages 67–73.

Liam Lonergan, Mengjie Qian, Neasa Ní Chiaráin, Christer Gobl, and Ailbhe Ní Chasaide. 2023b. Towards dialect-inclusive recognition in a low-resource language: are balanced corpora the answer? In *Proc. Interspeech 2023*, pages 5082–5086.

Min Ma, Yuma Koizumi, Shigeki Karita, Heiga Zen, Jason Riesa, Haruko Ishikawa, and Michiel Bacchiani. 2024. Fleurs-r: A restored multilingual speech corpus for generation tasks. In *Proc. Interspeech 2024*, pages 1835–1839.

Vimal Manohar, Hossein Hadian, Daniel Povey, and Sanjeev Khudanpur. 2018. Semi-supervised training of acoustic models using lattice-free MMI. In *2018 IEEE international conference on acoustics, speech and signal processing (ICASSP)*, pages 4844–4848. IEEE.

Andy Murphy, Liam Lonergan, Mengjie Qian, Harald Berthelsen, Christoph Wendler, Neasa Ní Chiaráin, Ailbhe Ní Chasaide, and Christer Gobl. 2023. Abair & Éist: a demonstration of speech technologies for Irish. In *2nd Annual Meeting of the ELRA/ISCA SIG on Under-resourced Languages (SIGUL 2023)*, pages 121–123.

Daniel Park, Yu Zhang, Ye Jia, Wei Han, Chung-Cheng Chiu, Bo Li, Yonghui Wu, and Quoc Le. 2020. Improved noisy student training for automatic speech recognition. In *Proc. Interspeech 2020*, pages 2817–2821.

Daniel S Park, William Chan, Yu Zhang, Chung-Cheng Chiu, Barret Zoph, Ekin D Cubuk, and Quoc V Le. 2015. Specaugment: A simple data augmentation method for automatic speech recognition. In *Proc. Interspeech 2015*, pages 2613–2617.

Vijayaditya Peddinti, Daniel Povey, and Sanjeev Khudanpur. 2025. A time delay neural network architecture for efficient modeling of long temporal contexts. In *Proc. Interspeech 2024*, pages 3214–3218.

Matt Post. 2018. A call for clarity in reporting BLEU scores. In *Proceedings of the Third Conference on Machine Translation: Research Papers*, pages 186–191, Belgium, Brussels. Association for Computational Linguistics.

Vasile Păiş and Dan Tufiş. 2022. Capitalization and punctuation restoration: a survey. *Artif. Intell. Rev.*, 55(3):1681–1722.

Mengjie Qian, Harald Berthelsen, Liam Lonergan, Andy Murphy, Claire O'Neill, Claire Ní Chiaráin, Christer Gobl, and Ailbhe Ní Chasaide. 2022. Automatic speech recognition for Irish: testing lexicons and language models. In *Proceedings of the 33rd Irish Signals and Systems Conference (ISSC)*, pages 1–6.

Alec Radford, Jong Wook Kim, Tao Xu, Greg Brockman, Christine McLeavey, and Ilya Sutskever. 2023. Robust speech recognition via large-scale weak supervision. In *International conference on machine learning*, pages 28492–28518. PMLR.

Peter Reichl, Sebastian Egger, Raimund Schatz, and Alessandro D'Alconzo. 2010. The logarithmic nature of QoE and the role of the Weber-Fechner law in QoE assessment. In *2010 IEEE International Conference on Communications*, pages 1–5. IEEE.

Team Silero. 2024. Silero VAD: pre-trained enterprise-grade Voice Activity Detector (VAD), Number Detector and Language Classifier. `https://github.com/snakers4/silero-vad`.

David Snyder, Daniel Garcia-Romero, Gregory Sell, Daniel Povey, and Sanjeev Khudanpur. 2018. X-vectors: Robust DNN embeddings for speaker recognition. In *2018 IEEE international conference on acoustics, speech and signal processing (ICASSP)*, pages 5329–5333. IEEE.

NLLB Team, Marta R. Costa-jussà, James Cross, Onur Çelebi, Maha Elbayad, Kenneth Heafield, Kevin Heffernan, Elahe Kalbassi, Janice Lam, Daniel Licht, Jean Maillard, Anna Sun, Skyler Wang, Guillaume Wenzek, Al Youngblood, Bapi Akula, Loic Barrault, Gabriel Mejia Gonzalez, Prangthip Hansanti, John Hoffman, Semarley Jarrett, Kaushik Ram Sadagopan, Dirk Rowe, Shannon Spruit, Chau Tran, Pierre Andrews, Necip Fazil Ayan, Shruti Bhosale, Sergey Edunov, Angela Fan, Cynthia Gao, Vedanuj Goswami, Francisco Guzmán, Philipp Koehn, Alexandre Mourachko, Christophe Ropers, Safiyyah Saleem, Holger Schwenk, and Jeff Wang. 2022. No language left behind: Scaling human-centered machine translation. *arXiv preprint arXiv:2005.09629*.

Ashish Vaswani, Noam Shazeer, Niki Parmar, Jakob Uszkoreit, Llion Jones, Aidan N Gomez, Ł ukasz Kaiser, and Illia Polosukhin. 2017. Attention is all you need. In *Advances in Neural Information Processing Systems*, volume 30. Curran Associates, Inc.

Yu Xi, Wen Ding, Kai Yu, and Junjie Lai. 2024. Semi-supervised learning for code-switching asr with large language model filter. *arXiv preprint arXiv:2407.04219*.

Hainan Xu, Tongfei Chen, Dongji Gao, Yiming Wang, Ke Li, Nagendra Goel, Yishay Carmiel, Daniel Povey, and Sanjeev Khudanpur. 2018. A pruned RNNLM lattice-rescoring algorithm for automatic speech recognition. In *2018 IEEE international conference on acoustics, speech and signal processing (ICASSP)*, pages 5929–5933. IEEE.

Yu Zhang, James Qin, Daniel Park, Wei Han, Chung-Cheng Chiu, Ruoming Pang, Quoc Le, and Yonghui Wu. 2020. Pushing the limits of semi-supervised learning for automatic speech recognition. *arXiv preprint arXiv:2010.10504*.

A Appendix: Additional Tables

	Full	Ul	Co	Mu	Nn
Syn	41.4	22.2	8.8	10.4	-
MG	17.3	3.1	5.6	3.4	5.2
SS	259.7	55.5	104.9	95.4	3.9
AB	36.6	10.3	2.5	14.6	9.2
CCh	25	-	25.0	-	-
BBhÁ	17.9	-	17.9	-	-
Total	**397.9**	**91.1**	**164.7**	**123.8**	**18.3**

Table 6: Duration breakdown in hours of ASR training set by speaker variety.

	Total Dur (h)	Ul	Co	Mu	Nn
MG	10.2	2.5	3.4	3.0	1.3
SS	28.2	7.5	10.4	10.3	-

Table 7: Duration breakdown by speaker variety of MíleGlór and Spontaneous Speech test sets.

	Dialect	Dur (h)
Adhmhaidin	Co	779.0
Barrscéalta	Ul	1002.4
Saol Ó Dheas	Mu	993.9
Nuacht	mix	400.0
Total	-	**3230.0**

Table 8: Duration in hours and dialect information of unsupervised set by radio show

	MG	SS	CV	FL	HL
#Utts	8,423	19,266	516	548	198
Dur (h)	10.2	28.2	0.6	2.2	0.7

Table 9: Number of utterances and total duration of test sets.

	#lines	#words	#chars
FO	1012	25772	163254
CV	515	3423	19617
FL	548	13634	86282
MG	8423	98463	559675

Table 10: Features of the databases used for evaluation

	#lines	#words	#chars
PC_ga	3.2	63.1	417.2
NCE	1.8	30.4	181.5
BI	0.3	0.8	4.5
SS	1.4	3.6	20.6

Table 11: Features of the databases used for training the Cap&Punct systems (numbers in millions)

Gaeilge Bhriste ó Shamhlacha Cliste: How Clever Are LLMs When Translating Irish Text?

Teresa Clifford
Fiontar & Scoil na Gaeilge
Dublin City University
ADAPT Centre
Dublin City University
teresa.clifford3@mail.dcu.ie

Abigail Walsh and Brian Davis
ADAPT Centre
Dublin City University
abigail.walsh@adaptcentre.ie
Brian.Davis@adaptcentre.ie

Micheál J. Ó Meachair
Fiontar & Scoil na Gaeilge
Dublin City University
micheal.omeachair@dcu.ie

Abstract

Large Language Models have been widely adopted in NLP tasks and applications, however, their ability to accurately process Irish and other minority languages has not been fully explored. In this paper we describe preliminary experiments examining the capacity of publicly-available machine translation engines (Google Translate, Microsoft Bing, and eTranslation) and prompt-based AI systems systems (ChatGPT 3.5, Llama 2) for translating and handling challenging language features of Irish. A hand-crafted selection of challenging Irish language features were incorporated into translation prompts, and the output from each model was examined by a human evaluator. The results of these experiments indicate that these LLM-based models still struggle with translating rare linguistic phenomena and ambiguous constructions. This preliminary analysis helps to inform further research in this field, providing a simple ranking of publicly-available models, and indicating which language features require particular attention when evaluating model capacity.

1 Introduction

The rising interest in transformer-based Large Language Models (LLMs) in the field of Natural Language Processing (NLP) can be seen in the high volume of publications continually being published in major computational linguistics venues year by year (e.g. LREC: (Ekgren et al., 2022); ACL: (Raunak et al., 2023), and (Wu and Hu, 2023); EACL: (Balloccu et al., 2024)), as well as increased use of ChatGPT and similar applications in people's daily lives. As hype surrounding these models continues to build with improvements in performance, the question arises of how the field of machine translation is impacted, and whether machine translation can be considered a 'solved problem' (Zhu et al., 2024).

Despite ongoing discussion, the field lacks depth of understanding on the ability of these models to process minority languages, including Irish. This paper describes preliminary experiments in order to shed light on the ability of publicly-available machine translation (MT) engines and prompt-based AI systems when translating certain hand-selected challenging features of the Irish language (e.g. non-compositional constructions such as *Bóín Dé* (God's little cow) 'ladybird').

Relevant background and related work is explored in Section 2, and Section 3 describes the experimental set up. The results of the experiments are recorded in Section 4, and include a human evaluation of the target translations. The experiments represent the initial steps in a thorough exploration of the capacity of LLM-based systems to process text from low-resourced languages such as Irish. Section 6 explores future areas for exploration in this research topic.

2 Background

2.1 Machine Translation for Irish

Irish is the official language of Ireland and an official EU language. Despite this status, the language is considered a low-resource language by European language researchers (Lynn, 2022), noted to have weak or no support in many categories of technological support for selected European languages, similar to West Frisian (Robinson-Jones and Scarse, 2022) and other minority languages. Lynn (2022) discusses how subpar applications and language

Proceedings of the 5th Celtic Language Technology Workshop (CLTW 5), pages 46–51
Abu Dhabi, UAE (Online), January 20, 2025

tools are a factor that can lead to Irish speakers switching to using English in online spaces, which contributes to the rising risk of digital extinction for the Irish language. To address this threat, the Department of Tourism, Culture, Arts, Gaeltacht, Sport and Media launched The Digital Plan for the Irish Language in December of 2022 (Ní Chasaide et al.). This plan calls attention to several areas of research that are vital to the advancement of Irish language technology, including Machine Translation (MT) and the development of key resources.

MT is an area of Irish language technology that has seen slow but relatively consistent development over past years, with publications demonstrating recent advances in the field, e.g. applying cutting edge methodology to building bidirectional English & Irish (EN<>GA) MT models (Lankford et al., 2024), and focusing on domain-specific translation (Lankford et al., 2021).

Irish is one of the languages supported by eTranslation (European Commission), an open-source MT platform developed in partnership with the European Commission. General-purpose MT systems, such as Google Translate (Google Research) and Microsoft Bing Translator (Microsoft Research), also offer support for the Irish language. Research group ABAIR (ABAIR) have developed applications with chatbot-style interactions primarily for Computer Assisted Language Learning (CALL) and grammar checking purposes; focusing on speech-to-text and text-to-speech technology (e.g. *An Scéalaí*[1], *An Bat Mírialta*[2]). However, it is difficult to assess the true capacity of many prompt-based AI systems to correctly handle Irish text. Some multi-lingual models (e.g. Gliglish)[3] may claim support for Irish language, but omit details on how the model has been trained, and what data was included in training. For example, when tested with Irish prompts, the Gliglish model showed substantial problems in the output, providing nonsensical replies (e.g. *Go raibh maith agat, táim ag cuir blasta ort agus beidh mé ag dul le... arán* meaning "Thank you, I am putting tasty on you and I will be going with... bread").

2.2 Translation Difficulty

Translation difficulty is often described in terms of human translators and their mental or cognitive load (Akbari and Segers, 2017; Sun, 2015). However, there is an overlap between the translation difficulty for human translators and MT systems (Vanroy et al., 2019). O'Brien (2004) examined the effect of **N**egative **T**ranslatability **I**ndicators (NTIs)—i.e. linguistic features that have been noted as problematic for MT (Gdaniec, 1994; Bernth, 1999; Bernth and Gdaneic, 2001; Underwood and Jongejan, 2001), such as the passive voice, and the gerund—on the post editing effort. The data suggested that the post-editing speed for sentences without NTIs was faster than those with them on average. Some of these NTIs, such as lexical ambiguity, also fall under the umbrella of translation ambiguity (Tokowicz, 2014). Examples of translation ambiguity can be seen in our tested language features (e.g. lexical ambiguity; one word having two meanings in one language).

3 Methodology

Experiments were set up to test the capacity of publicly-available MT engines and prompt-based AI models on translating certain hand-select NTIs, incorporated into translation examples and translation prompts in either English or Irish, based on the feature used for evaluation. Two rounds of experiments took place, with different translation examples selected for each round.

Six challenging features of the Irish language were selected for testing in Round One, with four additional features tested in Round Two. These features were chosen based on previous work on challenging features of Irish language (e.g. Walsh et al. (2019)), in research on translation difficulty in other languages (Tokowicz, 2014), and based on the the researchers' knowledge of the Irish language.

The features chosen for Round One were:

1. Words that have multiple meanings (e.g. homonyms "bark" the sound made by dogs vs "bark" the protective covering on trees)

2. Words that do not have direct translations in one language (e.g. *Súilaithne* means 'to know someone to see')

3. Non-compositional phrases, where the combined meanings of the individual words in a phrase are not equivalent to the meaning of the phrase (e.g. *Duilleog bháite* (drowned leaf) 'water lily')

4. Phrases including 'yes' and 'no', as there is no direct translation for these words in Irish

[1]https://scealai.abair.ie/
[2]https://bat-mirialta.abair.ie/
[3]https://gliglish.com/

5. Phrases using the construction 'I am', as there are two verbs for 'be' in Irish: copular and substantive 'be'

6. Uncensored swear words and innuendo (e.g. 'I fucked her')

The additional features included in Round Two were as follows:

7. *Logainmneacha* or Irish place names (e.g. *Baile Átha Cliath* 'Dublin')

8. *An tuiseal gairmneach* or the vocative case (e.g. *A **Sheáin*** features slenderisation and lenition in vocative case)

9. Non-compositional animal names (e.g. *Mac tíre* (son of the land) 'wolf')

10. Mythical creature names (e.g. *Bean Sí* (fairy woman) 'banshee')

The models chosen for Round One of these experiments were Google Translate (Google Research), Microsoft Bing Translator (Microsoft Research), eTranslation (European Commission) and ChatGPT 3.5 (OpenAI, 2024), with Llama 2 (Meta AI) being additionally included for the Round Two.[4] These applications were chosen as they are all publicly available, free to use,[5] and state that they can translate from English to Irish and Irish to English. This was assessed by the inclusion of Irish as one of the language options on the language list for MT applications, or by prompting the AI system, asking if it has the capability to translate English to Irish and vice versa. Prompt-based AI systems Gliglish and Gemini were originally considered for inclusion but were rejected due to their use cases not fitting the experiment parameters, with 1) Gliglish only accepting speech input, and 2) Gemini expressing it had the ability to translate to and from Irish when initially prompted in English, then stating it was unable to do so when asked directly to translate words or sentences provided in Irish. The applications were tested using default settings, with no changes to add advanced search features where these features were offered by the application.

[4]Models used were the most up-to-date version of the prompt-based AI systems at the time of the experiments.

[5]It should be noted that, while free to use, an account must be created to use eTranslation and ChatGPT.

Examples were hand-crafted words or sentences in Irish or English, integrating one of the listed features. New examples were crafted for Round Two, which integrated the additional language features and also new examples of the language features from Round One, often adjusted to include more specific context words, as informed by the research of Castilho and Knowles (2024) and Castilho et al. (2020) (e.g. Round One example: *Chonaic mé bóín Dé thíos ansin.* 'I saw a ladybird down there' vs. Round Two example: *Is feithid é bóín Dé* 'A lady bird is an insect'). Round One contained 57 examples, and Round Two contained 132 examples, for a total of 189 examples. Each example was manually fed into each system interface, and the outputs were recorded.

When collecting the translation outputs, only the first translation provided by each model was recorded, even when alternative translations were offered. Both ChatGPT 3.5 and Llama 2 were given the following initial prompt before the examples were provided: "Hello can you translate these sentences and words from English to Irish or from Irish to English please". Any extra context or information provided by the AI systems was also recorded.

4 Results

Given the range of potentially correct translations, a manual evaluation was deemed a more reliable means of capturing the models' capabilities rather than automatic metrics, e.g. BLEU. An assessment was made by a fluent Irish speaker to determine whether a target translation was 'plausible', i.e. a translation that may be incorrect due to the context of the example (i.e a direct translation of a non-compositional phrase) but there could be cases in which this translation is correct in context. 'High-quality' translations were those considered a correct and adequate translation, without grammatical error, and correct in context to the example. Table 1 displays the results of this assessment for the examples produced by each system, summed from Round One and Round Two. In Figure 1, the percentage of 'plausible' and 'high-quality' translations produced by each system are calculated for each feature, to indicate the general level of challenge each feature presents.

F3, F9, F10 exhibit the largest divide between 'plausible' and 'high-quality' translations. This suggests the systems are attempting to translate words

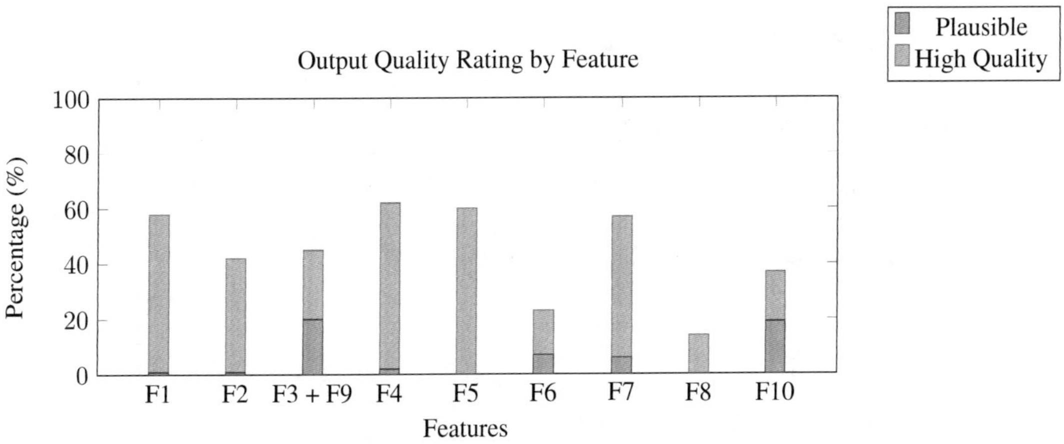

Figure 1: Percentage of 'plausible' and 'high-quality' translations per language feature. F1 stands for Feature 1, referring to the first of the features listed in Section 3. Non-compositional phrases (F3) and Non-compositional animal (F9) names were combined into F3 + F9.

System	Plausible	High-quality
Bing	51.3%	36.5%
Google	47.6%	38.1%
eTranslation	45%	32.3%
ChatGPT	46%	38.1%
Llama	28%	16%

Table 1: Percentage of 'plausible' and 'high-quality' translations for each system (rounded to the nearest decimal point) for both Round One and Round Two, out of a total of 189. Llama was used to test 132 examples, as it was not included in Round One.

System	Round One	Round 2	Both Rounds
Bing	51%	54%	52.5%
Google	47%	48%	47.5%
eTranslation	51%	42%	46.5%
ChatGPT	49%	45%	47%
Llama		28%	28%

Table 2: Rate of plausibility achieved by the systems in Round One, Round Two and across both rounds (rounded to the nearest decimal point).

that are out-of-vocabulary or rarely represented in the training data, leading to producing literal or word-for-word translations which could be classified as 'plausible' but not 'high-quality'. The issue of rare or out-of-vocabulary words may also be the case for F6, as swear words are likely filtered out of the training data. Similarly, with F8 and F10, mythical creatures and the vocative case may not be heavily represented in training data.

100% of the 'plausible' translations for features F5 and F8 were also 'high quality', which is intuitive as translations for these features can only be correct or incorrect. However, the rate of plausibility by systems for these features was only 60% and 14% respectively, indicating that systems struggled in particular with correct handling of the vocative case.

Table 2, provides the rate of plausibility achieved by each system over the different rounds of the experiments, to provide an overview of the system's capabilities to translate these features as a whole.

Microsoft Bing Translator was the most successful model for producing plausible translations of these challenging language features. Llama 2 was the least successful model overall. Of the models that were tested in both Rounds of the experiment, the eTranslation model was slightly less successful than the ChatGPT and Google models.

5 Conclusions

Despite having the highest rate of plausibility, Microsoft Bing Translator had an almost 50% rate of implausible translations. Even the features whose 'plausible' translations were all also 'high-quality', had rates of plausibility as low as 14%. From these initial experiments, it appears that LLMs and publicly-available MT models are currently not adequately supported for these challenging features of the Irish language, particularly for rare linguistic words and features, such as the vocative case, and swear words.

6 Future Work

Future experiments will aim to automate the input and prompting phase of the experiment, in order to increase the size of the test data. We also aim to include additional models (e.g. bespoke Irish encoder-decoder models, or other publicly-available models that support use of the Irish language). Additionally, we aim to expand the number of challenging language features explored; such as including culturally distinct words and phrases (e.g. 'foot path' in Ireland vs 'side walk' in the USA). Future experiments will include baseline examples, where each challenging feature is substituted with a non-challenging feature, in order to compare the capability of each model to translate a non-challenging example of the same syntactic or lexical form. Potential categorisation of the challenging features would help with this step (e.g. grouping lexically challenging examples, grammatically challenging examples, ambiguous examples), which will further inform the capacity of each model to handle different types of challenging language. Other experiment adjustments include prompting the AI systems systems in Irish as opposed to English.

7 Limitations

This research represents a preliminary study, exploring the results of including a small hand-crafted selection of examples of difficult-to-translate features of Irish.

A researcher with Irish language skills equivalent to a C2 level[6] developed the test set, and performed the analysis of the results. This limits the scope of the analysis. Words and phrases can have a variety of different meanings, and a single person cannot capture this variety. Not only could multiple researchers increase the likelihood of noticing any mistakes in typos in the test set, they would also hep ensure that valid translations that differ from one researcher's preferred translation would be captured. This would be particularly useful in the context of the Irish language, as a native speaker's dialect may influence what they would see as a correct translation.

These limitations acknowledged, these experiments provide an initial comparison of systems for automatic translation, indicates particularly problematic features that require more investigation, and leaves room for future experiments incorporating these insights and adjusted methodology.

[6]According to CEFR Levels provided here: https://www.coe.int/en/web/common-european-framework-reference-languages/table-1-cefr-3.3-common-reference-levels-global-scale

Acknowledgments

eSTÓR's ongoing operations and growth are sustained through funding from the Department of Tourism, Culture, Arts, Gaeltacht, Sport and Media. We would also like to thank the reviewers for their detailed feedback, many of whose comments were incorporated into the final paper.

References

ABAIR. Abair.ie. https://abair.ie/ga.

Alireza Akbari and Winibert Segers. 2017. Translation Difficulty: How to Measure and What to Measure. *Lebende Sprachen*, pages pp. 3–29.

Simone Balloccu, Patrícia Schmidtová, Mateusz Lango, and Ondrej Dusek. 2024. Leak, Cheat, Repeat: Data Contamination and Evaluation Malpractices in Closed-Source LLMs. In *Proceedings of the 18th Conference of the European Chapter of the Association for Computational Linguistics (Volume 1: Long Papers*, pages 67–93, St. Julian's, Malta. Association for Computational Linguistics.

Arendse Bernth. 1999. A confidence index for Machine Translation. In *Proceedings of the 8th Conference on Theoretical and Methodological Issues in Machine Translation of Natural Languages*, University College, Chester.

Arendse Bernth and Claudia Gdaneic. 2001. MTranslatabilityy. *Machine Translation, Volume 16, Issue 3*, pages pp. 175–218.

Sheila Castilho and Rebecca Knowles. 2024. A survey of context in neural machine translation and its evaluation. *Natural Language Processing*, pages pp. 1–31.

Sheila Castilho, Maja Popović, and Andy Way. 2020. On Context Span Needed for Machine Translation Evaluation. In *Proceedings of the Twelfth Language Resources and Evaluation Conference*, pages pp. 3735–3742, Marseille, France. European Language Resources Association.

Ariel Ekgren, Amaru Cuba Gyllensten, Evangelia Gogoulou, Alice Heiman, Severine Verlinden, Joey Öhman, Fredrik Carlsson, and Magnus Sahlgren. 2022. Lessons Learned from GPT-SW3: Building the First Large-Scale Generative Language Model for Swedish. In *Proceedings of the Thirteenth Language Resources and Evaluation Conference*, pages 3509–3518, Marseille, France. European Language Resources Association.

European Commission. eTranslation - The European Commission's Machine Translation System. https://commission.europa.eu/resources-partners/etranslation_en.

Claudia Gdaniec. 1994. The Logos Translatability Index. In *Proceedings of the First Conference of the Association for Machine Translation in the Americas*, Columbia, Maryland, USA.

Google Research. Google Translate. https://translate.google.com/?sl=en&tl=ga&op=translate.

Seamus Lankford, Haithem Afli, and Andy Way. 2021. Machine Translation in the Covid domain: an English-Irish case study for LoResMT 2021. In *Proceedings of the 4th Workshop on Technologies for MT of Low Resource Languages (LoResMT2021)s*, pages 144–150, Virtual. Association for Machine Translation in the Americas.

Séamus Lankford, Haithem Afli, and Andy Way. 2024. Design of an open-source architecture for neural machine translation. *arXiv preprint arXiv:2403.03582*.

Teresa Lynn. 2022. Report on the Irish language. https://european-language-equality.eu/deliverables/. Technical Report D1.20, European Language Equality Project.

Meta AI. Llama. https://www.llama.com/llama2/.

Microsoft Research. Microsoft Bing Translator. https://www.bing.com/Translator/.

Ailbhe Ní Chasaide, Neasa Ní Chiarán, Elaine Uí Dhonnchadha, Teresa Lynn, and John Judge. Digital Plan for the Irish Language Speech and Language Technologies 2023-2027. Available at https://assets.gov.ie/241755/e82c256a-6f47-4ddb-8ce6-ff81df208bb1.pdf.

Sharon O'Brien. 2004. Machine Translatability and Post-Editing Effort: How do they relate. In *Proceedings of Translating and the Computer 26*, London, UK. Aslib.

OpenAI. 2024. ChatGPT (November 29 version) [Large language model]. https://chatgpt.com/.

Vikas Raunak, Amr Sharaf, Yiren Wang, Hany Awadalla, and Arul Menezes. 2023. Leveraging GPT-4 for Automatic Translation Post-Editing. In *Findings of the Association for Computational Linguistics: EMNLP 2023"*, pages 12009–12024, Singapore. Association for Computational Linguistics.

Charlie Robinson-Jones and Ydwine Scarse. 2022. *Report on the West Frisian Language (Language Technology Support of Europe's Languages in 2020/2021 - European Language Equality project)*.

Sanjun Sun. 2015. Measuring translation difficulty: Theoretical and methodological considerations. *Across Languages and Cultures*, pages pp. 29–54.

Natasha Tokowicz. 2014. Translation ambiguity affects language processing, learning, and representation. In *Selected Proceedings of the 2012 Second Language Research Forum*, pages pp. 170–180.

Nancy Underwood and Bart Jongejan. 2001. Translatability checker: a tool to help decide whether to use MT. In *Proceedings of Machine Translation Summit VIII*, Santiago de Compostela, Spain.

Bram Vanroy, Orphée De Clerq, and Lieve Macken. 2019. Correlating process and product data to get an insight into translation difficulty. *ERSPECTIVES-STUDIES IN TRANSLATION THEORY AND PRACTICE*, pages pp. 924–941.

Abigail Walsh, Teresa Lynn, and Jennifer Foster. 2019. Ilfhocail: A lexicon of Irish MWEs. *Proceedings of the Joint Workshop on Multiword Expressions and WordNet (MWE-WN 2019)*, pages pp. 162–168.

Yangjian Wu and Gang Hu. 2023. Exploring Prompt Engineering with GPT Language Models for Document-Level Machine Translation: Insights and Findings. In *Proceedings of the Eighth Conference on Machine Translation*, pages 166–169, Singapore. Association for Computational Linguistics.

Wenhao Zhu, Hongyi Liu, Qingxiu Dong, Jingjing Xu, Shujian Huang, Lingpeng Kong, Jiajun Chen, and Lei Li. 2024. Multilingual machine translation with large language models: Empirical results and analysis. In *Findings of the Association for Computational Linguistics: NAACL 2024*, pages 2765–2781, Mexico City, Mexico. Association for Computational Linguistics.

Author Index